MINDING YOUR GOLF

The Game, Them and <u>YOU</u>

Four Winds Publications Ltd
7, 13 Tavistock Place
London WC1H 9SH
England

First published in Great Britain by Four Winds Publications 1998

Design and Layout by Wellset Repro.
Printed and bound in Great Britain by
Biddles Ltd Book Manufacturers, Guildford

ISBN 0 9534024 0 1

MINDING YOUR GOLF

The Game, Them and YOU

VARDA LEYMORE

Illustrations by Eldad Druks

Four Winds Publications
London

CONTENTS

LIST OF FIGURES

Introduction

The French say that golf is not a game, but a self-inflicted mental torment. With some it becomes an obsession. And it is certainly addictive. Golf is a game that hooks and does not let go even the poorest player. It is a source of agony and ecstasy, a perpetual challenge and a supreme reward. On good days it seems easy; on bad days it is hell. Thinking and remembering are both very bad for the game. Past glories can never be matched again, but problems cling. Every golfer knows the sinking feeling in the pit of the stomach when stepping onto the tee of a torturing hole. One tries hard to keep the memories at bay and the emotions under firm control, but to no avail. Then one day, for no particular reason, something good happens, and for a while the hole behaves as loyally as a dog.

I have learnt to play golf relatively late in life. To be precise, I was in my mid-thirties, and with a child. As though that was not enough, I was recovering from a car accident that left me 15% invalid. My doctor was a keen golfer and a strong believer in the Greek philosophy of a healthy mind in a healthy body. He recommended golf as an ideal occupation for a woman in my condition. It was not an auspicious start.

We were living abroad at the time and my first teacher was a Nigerian. He was a tall Yoruba man with a graceful body and an elegant natural swing. His mind was uncluttered and he had never had a golf lesson in his life. He learnt to play golf from caddying for the 'master'. The first thing he told me in his earnest sort of way was, that I would need three lessons to learn to play golf: One lesson for irons, one lesson for woods, and one lesson for bunkers and putting. Not knowing any better, I believed him. Some months later, I was still blaming my 'condition' for not being able to master the technique more quickly.

There are two misconceptions about golf among the uninitiated. First, that it is a game like any other game: that it needs to be learnt, and once learnt, one will know how to play it. Any golfer will testify from bitter experience that this is not the case. Golf is an elusive game. Like a *femme fatale* one never knows when it will betray you.

The second misconception about golf is the belief that one was singled out to have this constant struggle with the game, while the rest of the world finds it easier. To discover that all golfers, even top internationals, fall prey from time to time to the same embarrassments and humiliations as oneself, is an invigorating revelation. "Try the driver," a spectator mocked Tom Kite from the gallery, after the golfer made several wretched attempts to get his ball out of a bunker.

If golf were a mirror, the whole complexity of human nature would be reflected in it. Anything can affect the quality of the game, but just how is a guess. Golf defies prediction and the same conditions are more likely than not to produce wildly contradictory results. If your husband took off with a woman half his age, you would naturally be devastated. You would feel let down and betrayed: vulnerable financially and socially. You would stand over the ball with a heart full of hatred and eyes bleary with tears. Thus distressed, you may play poorly which is understandable, but equally well, you may play divinely.

If there is one irrefutable principle in golf, it is that unpredictability is the essence of the game. You may practice every day and hit absolutely wonderful shots on the driving range, but once on the golf course, everything is different. People are watching. The ball hits a tree and ends up in a ditch. You have an air shot and begin to feel hot under the collar. Meanwhile, your opponent has two regular shots to the green and stands there, waiting patiently with an aura of studied nonchalance. "Bad luck!" He cries full of solicitude, and "You were robbed!" when, as a final humiliation, the ball circles the hole and does not drop.

When one plays golf, one must be prepared to be cruelly humbled without losing heart. One must accept punishment with a thin smile and have faith in a brighter future. For at some unknown point in time, when it is least expected and capitulation seems imminent, the game returns in all its glory.

This book is written for the club player. It discusses the main topics in Sport Psychology which are relevant to golf. The material is designed to furnish the player with an understanding of the psychological mechanisms underlying common situations on the golf course, and with the means to combat the torments of this enchanting game.

The book starts with the discussion of character, the single most important factor in the game. In golf, one does not have technical problems, one has personality problems. The chapter on pitfalls and snares outlines the most common psychological obstructions which prevent the player from achieving his true potential. It covers the issues of personality types, anxiety, rage, confidence, arousal, control, the need-for-achievement and the fear-of-failure. What to do and how to cope in a crisis is examined in the chapter on survival strategies. The book then goes on to discuss the delights and horrors of playing with good guys and rogues, and the special considerations of playing with men as partners and as opponents. It finally looks at matchplay and at winners and losers.

1: Learning To Play

Informed opinion claims that only two aspects of the swing can be learnt: the grip and the stance. The rest is 'feel'. It does not matter who teaches you to play, though it is best to avoid absolute pirates. Whoever the instructor is, you will develop your own personal style, and you had better stick with it. To struggle against what comes naturally and, instead, attempt to emulate an idea of perfection is an exercise in futility. You may spend months, labouring to model your swing on Seve Ballesteros or Nick Faldo, and it may even work for a while, but it will not last. In the fullness of time you will realise that your swing is just that: **your** own, and it suits you best. To struggle against it will condemn you to years of frustration. It is far better to work with your natural swing than against it. Some years ago, in an inter-county match, a large lady arrived on the tee. She was tall and broad and powerfully built, but those were not the reasons why all eyes were glued to her. When she addressed the ball, she squatted at a 90° angle in a manner strongly reminiscent of a posture in another place. We struggled to control our mirth. To hit a ball from that position seemed impossible. But she did, and the ball flew long and straight to the pin with tantalising regularity. She won the match.

A fortune is spent on tuition in the hope of achieving greatness. The single most important ingredient in successful instruction is the faith that you have in your pro. Very few people can persevere with something that feels awkward and has horrendous results to start with. Nick Faldo did it, but how many Nick Faldos are there?

Faldo spent two torturous years rebuilding his swing, and the results were indeed spectacular. In a television interview he was asked about his new caddy, Fanny Sunneson, the only woman who caddies for a top player, who is not her husband. Nowadays Fanny is an integral part of the professional tour, but nine years ago she was something of a novelty.

"What does a player of your calibre do with a woman caddy?" the interviewer asked Faldo quizzically. It was a sly question and he raised his eyebrows to emphasise the Ha, Ha point.

Faldo reflected carefully before he made a revealing reply: "She understands my swing," he answered gravely. Mind you, not, "She understands **me**," but, "She understands **my swing!**" In other words, I am my swing, or better still: I swing, therefore, I am.

After the big successes came the trough. Two years later, and still relatively in the doldrums, even Faldo decided, "to return to a more natural swing." Ballesteros, the man with the most poetic swing in the world, was going through a very bad patch. He lost his touch, and the game that once was a sugar puff became an instrument of torture. He decided to go mechanical and swing the Leadbetter way. It did not work. His game was ruined and so was his back. Greg Norman worked hard to correct his swing. It took him, in his words to: "another level ... about five levels down from where I'd been."

- **Conclusion:** *Make the most of your own swing:*
  it is the only one you have got.

In a sense, one never learns to play golf. Or rather, one never stops learning. It is an ongoing never-ending process. Jack Nicklaus in his mid-forties summed it up succinctly: "I'm still learning to play golf," said the man who is considered to be the greatest golfer ever. The more one knows, the more aware one is of the pitfalls, and the harder it is to play well. A state of innocence is ideal but, unfortunately, cannot be maintained. The game surrenders some of its secrets, but never reveals all its devilish ways.

On the face of it, the golf swing is simplicity itself. Assuming that the head is kept still and the arm straight, all one does is draw a circle in the air. In this circle, the head is the centre and the arm is the radius. Euclidean geometry is a science for Pete's sake, and in theory, it is impossible to miss a shot, but plenty of theoretically unmissable shots, are missed. There must be good reasons for these mishaps, and those who follow the mechanical school of thinking in golf will advance them with great conviction. But how then will one account for the fact, that the same person with apparently the same swing will play sublimely one day and dreadfully the next day? What makes the game change dramatically in mid-course? Surely, not a sudden collapse in ability, or knowledge. The answer is in the mind and the only probe into it, imperfect as it may be, is psychology.

2: Pitfalls and Snares

"Character is destiny," said Heraclitus. What is that elusive thing called character? Inner grit? Fighting spirit? Loser mentality? The most dangerous enemy in golf is the enemy within. That beast of prey which lies in wait ready to pounce on you like a bolt from the blue. But that is only half the story. When the chips are down, nothing counts more than character. "A man is not licked till he quits," memorably proclaimed Burt Lancaster in The Birdman of Alcatraz. One loses first in one's mind and only then on the ground.

> *I once played a match against a man who was three up with four holes to go. On the fifteenth, his tee shot flew through a narrow valley and landed on a rocky mound. There it clung like a beetle, held up by the softest of moss. "How the hell can it stay up there?" I overheard him grumble in exasperation. Hitting a ball clinging to a rock at eye level without damaging your club or causing yourself grievous bodily harm, takes some doing. He rose to the challenge and missed. Gritting his teeth, he tried again and chipped his club. That maddened him. "Hell, I'm done for...," he murmured in a stunned sort of way. He was an eight-handicapper and fully capable of still winning the match. But, no, he gave up and lost.*

Why should one's psyche turn against oneself? The laws of nature are based on instinct for self-preservation, not for self-destruction. Why is it that in golf, negative thoughts come to haunt the player with obdurate persistence? Certain bunkers, ditches and lakes regularly interfere with one's play though they can easily be avoided. In *The Inner Game of Golf,* Timothy Gallwey suggests that a hostile ego whispers in one's ear like a Iago out to persecute Desdemona's alleged lover.

The literature on the psychology of sport is silent on this matter, possibly because it is more characteristic of golf than any other game.

The enemy within …

- In no other sport does the player have such abundance of time to reflect and consult on what to do, and then do it at one's leisure.

- In no other sport is the time lag between units of action longer.

- In no other game is the action so brief in relation to the total time required to complete a round. At a conservative four seconds per shot, an average player needs approximately six minutes to play eighteen holes, just about 2.5% of the total time he spends on the course.

Is it surprising that the mind wanders and that it is difficult to remain focused? What qualities do we need to command our own actions? Why is it so excruciatingly difficult to do what we so desperately want to do? Why are we self-destructive?

Over the years many attempts have been made to understand these critical issues. The greatest minds pondered and puzzled over the bewildering jungle of human nature. And the debate is still raging.

Sport psychology targets the problems which plague performance on the battle field of sport. Of these, none is more important than anxiety.

ANXIETY

Anxiety is the single most insidious and debilitating factor in poor performance. One can survive fever, chest infection, a broken leg, but not a serious attack of nerves. In short, anxiety on (and off) the golf course is a curse.

The first thing to understand about anxiety is that it is not an aberration or some kind of shameful weakness. On the contrary, it is a genetically evolved mechanism which is absolutely essential for survival. Anxiety is triggered by a threat to the safety of ego, and it works by sending an alert signal to the brain. This activates the sympathetic division of the autonomic nervous system and prepares it for *fight* or *flight*.

The nervous system is immensely complicated. The chart overleaf presents only its bare essentials. It reveals at a glance just how little of what is going on in our body and mind we consciously control. Ego may think that he is the boss, but he is not. Its sphere of influence is strictly limited. We exercise direct control only over the voluntary muscles, which are the somatic division of the EFFERENT division of the **peripheral** nervous system.

The body is sovereign and functions pretty well, indeed better, thank you, without interference from ego. It is virtually impossible to impose our will on the autonomous functions of the body, though there are roundabout ways to coax them into declaring a temporary truce. A golfer's best bet is to concentrate his mind as best he can and let the body do the rest.

Of course, no one in his right mind bolts from the golf course in mortal fear, nor do golfers often come to blows. The most common reaction to an attack of nerves in golf is *flight* or *freeze*. Anxiety penetrates the mind like a silent scream. The game collapses along with the will to fight. Muscle tension in the neck, shoulders, stomach, arms and legs builds up and makes every shot a missile into the unknown. "It was a nightmare," a four-handicapper succinctly summed up her ordeal on the course.

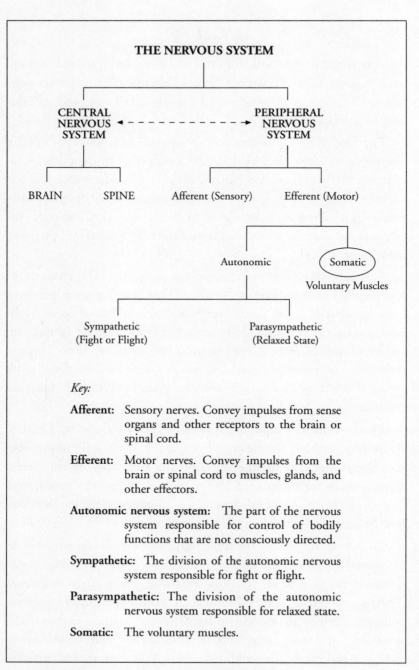

Figure 1. The Nervous System

Recent research on anxiety revealed that it plagues sportsmen more than the rest of the population. Like models and actors, they are narcissistic and worry incessantly about their body and their performance. But golfers are less susceptible to bouts of apprehension than are other sportsmen. Their anxiety threshold is significantly higher than, say, tennis players, athletes or high jumpers. However, when an attack of nerves rears its treacherous head, the result can be, and often is, devastating.

There are two types of anxiety:

- **trait anxiety,**
  and
- **state anxiety.**

Trait anxiety is an inborn quality of character and, therefore, a constant factor in one's personality. **State anxiety** is precipitated only in threatening situations. Certain conditions provoke it. I do not know whether Bernard Langer is a particularly anxious character by nature, but the last putt – the one upon which the result of the 1991 Ryder Cup depended – on the crocodile infested course in Kiawah Island, surely made him feel very anxious indeed, and not because of the crocodiles.

Trait anxiety is a given quality, like having blue eyes or dark hair. Some people are born more anxious than others, and some are born with a sunny disposition. There is not much that can be done about the born worriers, but state anxiety is a variable that can be manipulated. More to the point, it affects performance far more than the propensity to be anxious. Sport psychology concentrates on state anxiety, because this is an area where it can make a useful contribution.

State anxiety is not a matter of objective evaluation and has very little to do with a rational assessment of any given situation. It depends entirely upon the individual's subjective perception of something as stressful or threatening. The strength of the reaction reflects the interaction between the person's anxiety potential and various stressors in the environment. Naturally, the higher the anxiety potential, the higher the state anxiety in competitive situations.

There are two components in state anxiety:

- **worry,**
  and
- **emotionality.**

Worry is the result of reasoned analysis of the situation. It reflects the cognitive elements of anxiety, including legitimate concerns about one's preparedness for the match, ability to cope with the tension and the potential consequences of defeat. It is caused by negative expectations and poor self-image. Worry is conscious and rational, and expresses itself in obsessive self-analysis, often accompanied by vivid images of disaster and premonitions of doom and gloom. If the player is already unsure of himself, worry exacerbates matters considerably.

Emotionality (= somatic anxiety) reflects the physiological aspect of anxiety and the physical symptoms of tensing up. It is displayed in tense muscles, butterflies in the stomach, pounding heart, difficulties in breathing and a squeaky voice. The main components of anxiety are summarised in Figure 2.

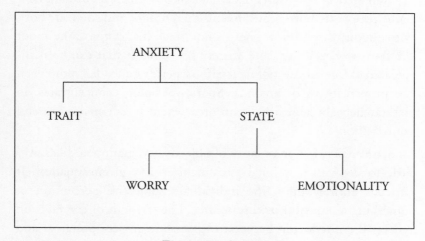

Figure 2. Anxiety

In golf, as in other sports which call for high levels of cognitive thinking, worry is a major obstacle to performance. The mind is diverted by thoughts and emotions which are not relevant to the task in hand. Instead of concentrating on the shots, the golfer becomes preoccupied with peripheral matters, predominantly those that seem to confirm his apprehensions. An innocent giggle is interpreted as mocking. Innocuous remarks are suspiciously probed as though they were coded messages. An embarrassing memory returns to haunt the player, just as he attempts a crucial putt. The more the mind thrashes about out of focus, the worse will he play. The more obsessive the need to win, the more threatening the situation becomes. The resulting poor shots reinforce his perception of imminent disaster and the downward spiral is set to accelerate.

Anxiety ...

A high state anxiety spells a crisis in the mental disposition of the player. It may be initiated by something quite trivial: a missed putt, a wayward shot, and the most dreaded of all: a sudden shank. They affect the golfer both mentally and physically. Without going into the intricate subject of myology, suffice it to say that an anxious golfer utilises far too much energy. The enhanced flow of adrenaline causes the activation of muscles unnecessary for the shot as well as over-tautness in the participating muscles. This is why the shots are powerful, but their direction defies prediction. I remember one case when the golfer was so tense that he hit a convoluted shot which made the ball fly backwards, not forwards. A calmer golfer uses less energy. The activation and, equally important, the relaxation of the non-participating muscles, are far more efficient. This is what gives top golfers the appearance of effortless smooth swing.

The effect of trait anxiety on performance was extensively researched by Weinberg. He discovered that too much anxiety harms performance, a finding that did not raise any eyebrows. Rather more surprisingly, he found that too little anxiety is also not good. Moderate levels of anxiety, like stage fright, keep the players on their toes, elevate their performance to new heights and produce best results.

Is it possible to control anxiety? The short answer is yes and no.

- **Yes,** because the early awareness of the coming onslaught serves as a security buffer and gives the player a small leeway to exercise self-defence. Recognising the first symptoms of anxiety and developing ways of dealing with them are invaluable assets in stressful situations. The more experienced a player is, the better he will know how to handle himself when the going gets tough.

- **No,** because beyond a certain point on the roller coaster of crisis, the plain truth is that nothing can be done to save the situation on the day.

SUMMARY 1: ANXIETY

1. The body is its own master. Ego has very little control over what is happening in the body.

2. Anxiety is a natural reaction of the organism to a threatening situation, and prepares it for fight or flight. It is 'good' in small doses and crippling in big ones.

3. Trait anxiety is a given aspect of oneself, like height or being good at maths. It describes the extent to which one is prone to being anxious.

4. State anxiety is triggered by the individual's **subjective** perception of a situation as stressful or threatening.

5. State anxiety has two components:
   - worry – the cognitive aspect, and
   - emotionality – the physiological aspect.

6. State anxiety affects performance more than the propensity to be anxious.

CONFIDENCE

Confidence is everything. It is the single most powerful predictor of performance. A confident golfer perceives even stressors with glee. They become a challenge, a source of inspiration rather than a handicap.

According to Martens there are three types of players:

- **The diffident,** who is plagued by the self-fulfilling prophecy: He expects to lose and therefore does lose.

- **The confident,** who believes in himself. He handles mistakes well, reacts constructively and focuses on the task in hand.

- **The overconfident.** This is the cocky player. One or two mistakes are enough to puncture this hot air balloon.

Everyone wants to win from time to time, but some players are consistently more successful than others. Hard work and ability are very important but are not enough to explain success. That has something to do with the player's self-concept.

Self-concept is the set of views which the individual has about himself. It is a composite of his:

- **Self-image,** which is what he knows about himself.

- **Self-esteem,** which is how he feels about himself.
- **Ideal-self,** which is what he would like to be.

The closer the ideal-self is to the self-image, the higher is the self-esteem.

Self-esteem is the power broker which eggs one on to heroic endeavours, or puts paid to wild ambition. It is the cardinal factor in both the selection of a goal and the determination to achieve it. These two things: commitment to the goal and its perceived difficulty are important factors in ultimate success. Players with high self-esteem double their efforts to achieve the goal when it is hard. Low-self-esteemers are quitters. When the going gets tough, they are inclined to give up. It cannot be emphasised too strongly that someone who has a low self-esteem is not necessarily a bad player. In fact, he may be a terrific player with a personality problem that needs to be addressed in order to liberate him from his shackles. It is alleged that John Daly is a quitter, and that this was the reason Tom Watson did not include him in the American team of the Ryder Cup. It explains, however, why such a fantastic player does not win more often.

Confidence is a measure of the individual's belief in himself. It underpins what one chooses to do, how hard one works at it and how long one perseveres in face of difficulties. High confidence is a character trait, but how certain can one be to perform well in specific, often unknown and volatile situations like a golf competition, is another matter. The gauge which measures one's confidence in one's ability to cope in specific situations is **self-efficacy.** Four factors contribute to high self-efficacy:

1. A record of past accomplishments: The more one wins, the more likely is one to continue to win.

2. Comparison of self with others: If they can do it, I can do it. Whatever they can do, I can do better.

3. Persuasion by credible others: If they think I can do it – I can.

4. Self-perception of readiness (optimal emotional arousal).

Those who score high on self-efficacy have a sense of being in command. This automatically reduces stress and acts as a positive feedback on their performance. Confidence is also a cardinal factor in one's ability to function well when others are watching. The more confident one is and the harder the task, the better will one perform under observation. The joy of playing to the gallery inevitably means that **evaluation apprehension** – the concern about what others think of us – is small. Being the centre of attention becomes a tonic rather than a hindrance. A particularly important determinant of confidence is the player's track record: the more victories under one's belt, the more confident will one be of success.

How to become more self-confident?

- Be honest. Take a hard look at yourself and try to assess as objectively as you can how good you really are. What are your weaknesses? What are your strengths?

- Set yourself specific targets. Make a plan how to achieve them. **P&P:** Practise and persevere.

- Practise positive thinking. Remind yourself of your strengths. Remember past glories.

- Seek and **accept** encouragement from significant others.

RAGE

Rage, like anxiety, is precipitated by threat. Unlike anxiety, the predominant reaction to anger is **fight** rather than flight. If anxiety causes one to crumble inwardly, fury is invigorating by its very nature. It demands an attack on an external agent, be it only an innocent bystander, the course, the 'guilty' club and even oneself. The effect is energising rather than freezing. Anger is less crippling than anxiety because it provides a target for attack while anxiety reduces the player to an inert bundle of nerves.

Aggression is different from rage. Silva distinguishes three types of aggression:

- **Hostile aggression** is motivated by *anger* with intent to harm.
- **Instrumental aggression** is motivated by a *desire to win* and is tinged with an intent to harm.
- **Assertive aggression** is the use of *legitimate force and strategy* to achieve a goal.

Rage is a form of hostile aggression. It focuses attention on harming the opponent and diverts precious resources away from the task in hand. When Mike Tyson bit off part of his opponent's ear, he vented his frustration, but he did not win the match. Rage is, in effect, a form of neurotic coping. Like a palace revolution, it turns against its master and destroys from within any possibility of effective action. Energy is dissipated in emotional turmoil and concentration is wrecked beyond repair.

Rage ...

Instrumental and especially assertive aggression are often conducive to better performance. They galvanise the player into action, stiffen the determination to fight and physically increase the flow of energy to the muscles.

Why is anger an unacceptable emotion on the golf course? After all, there is plenty of frustration to contend with. In professional tournaments rage is taboo. That is why Colin Montgomerie, Ronan Rafferty and John Daly do stand out, though their outbursts are mild by comparison with McEnroe, who in his own inimitable way immortalised the combustible tennis player. It is one thing, presumably, to watch McEnroe castigating the umpire, and quite another to see golfers bare their inner demons in public. The former is comical and certainly entertaining, while the latter is merely embarrassing.

Club golfers, especially beginners, give vent to their rage by mutilating the course or uttering expletive deletives. This conduct unbecoming acts as a safety valve and grants the player a momentary relief. It cannot and will not restore equanimity. Indeed, since anger is cumulative, one explosion leads to another as the frustration and humiliation fuel the buildup. The difference between the infantile and grown-up golfer is that the former erupts in a series of tantrums while the latter seethes in frustration.

EXTRAVERTS AND INTROVERTS

The personality dimension extraversion-introversion was first identified by the eminent psychologist, Hans Eysenck, some thirty years ago. In the fad-ridden world of psychology ideas come and go, but this construct has proved to be exceptionally enduring. In it several important traits consistently combine to produce a coherent personality type.

Extraverts are chronically under-aroused. To be happy and stimulated, they need company and constant activity. They are gregarious, dominant, aggressive, adventurous and socially dependent. Introverts are over-aroused and seek peace. They tend to be aloof, serious, shy, modest and self-sufficient. The extraverts need more external stimulation, and function best in a stimuli-rich environment. They are thick-skinned and not easily upset. Introverts have richer inner lives and require less external stimulation.

To achieve contentment, extraverts need high doses of excitation, while introverts are just as content with less. Because extraverts are 'reducers' and introverts are 'augmenters', the same sensation, say pain, feels stronger to the introvert than to the extravert. Introverts are happy in a relatively monotonous environment, and can sustain sensory deprivation far better than the extraverts. Introverts are inner-directed and seek approval by their own stringent standards. They respond better to praise. Extraverts are other-directed and need to have the approval and admiration of others. They respond better to blame.

What do these distinctions have to do with golf? From a psychological point of view – everything. The accepted wisdom was that outgoing, extravert personalities do better in sports than shy and introverted people. This view was inspired chiefly by the 'spectators factor', and the conviction that extraverts thrive on being the centre of attention while introverts shy away from the glare of the limelight. Subsequent research revealed that things are considerably more complex than that, and much depends on the type of sport in question.

- **Introverts** do better in individualistic, self-pacing sports which take place in monotonous environment and are time consuming. Golf, archery, long-distance running and mountain climbing are prime examples.

- **Extraverts** do well in team sports in fast changing environment, eg soccer, basketball, rugby.

However, when it comes to excellence as distinct from the merely high standard, introverts have a better chance of success, no matter what kind of sport they engage in. This surprising finding was confirmed in a study of top international sportsmen. The advantage of the introvert over the extravert is precisely the ability to detach from surroundings and focus on the task in hand. The reason some outstanding sportsmen seem tongue-tied is, that they are essentially shy, ie introverts.

Hardman researched several important character attributes in sportsmen and compared their scores to the population average. His findings proved a fascinating mixture of the expected and the unexpected. Not surprisingly, sportsmen had particularly high scores on independence as opposed to submissiveness. They were aggressive, domineering, daring, decisive and preferred activities which gratify these inclinations. Emotionally, they tended to be unstable and exceedingly self-centred. The sporty personality scored high on competitiveness, enthusiasm and cheerfulness, and poorly on maturity and hardheadedness. There were remarkably high scores on irresponsibility, suspicion and envy, as well as great intolerance of criticism.

The findings in other respects were even more revealing. For example, sportsmen engaged in surprisingly high levels of abstract thinking, and the results of their IQ tests were consistently higher than the population average. Top internationals did consistently better than other sportsmen.

THE NEED-FOR-ACHIEVEMENT (NFA) *AND THE FEAR-OF-FAILURE* (FoF)

The Need-for-Achievement is a basic character trait. It cannot be learnt and it cannot be satisfied. It manifests itself in restless energy and drive. Richard Branson has it in abundance. "I want to conquer the world," proclaimed Madonna, aged nineteen and armed 'only' with her talent, looks and indomitable will. All the great champions are insatiable; there is always another peak to climb. The Need-for-Achievement is characterised by:

- The will to succeed,
- Commitment to persevere,
- Action-doer mentality rather than day-dreaming.

McClelland and Atkinson have developed a mathematical model which shows that the Need-for-Achievement is highest when the probability of success is exactly 50%.

In stroke play (or stableford) the aim is to have the fewest possible shots. Safety play and the need to avoid trouble are paramount considerations. There is no need for fireworks, and it is often better to take a quiet penalty shot than make a desperate attempt to extricate oneself from trouble.

In matchplay, on the other hand, the only objective is to play slightly better than the opponent. To have a birdie when the other is struggling with a double bogey is not the best utilisation of scarce resources. When in trouble, suicidal shots rarely cost, as the hole is already as good as lost. If there is the slightest chance that they might work, they ought to be attempted. When Paul Azinger took a three-iron to play his third shot to the eighteenth hole at the Belfry, there was an audible gasp in the commentators' box. He was playing against Seve Ballesteros in the 1989 Ryder cup and he was one up. His tee shot ended in the water, that was the tomb of so many American balls. Unlike anyone else, he elected to drop the ball under the trees, not far from the treacherous stream. The ball had to fly low and far over the fairway and over two notorious water hazards to reach the green. To attempt it was sheer madness, but Ballesteros had a good tee shot and Azinger had to try it, for if he did not, the hole was surely lost, and the match halved. The ball landed in a green-side bunker, not on the green, but it was enough to unnerve Ballesteros to such an extent that he put his ball in the water in front of the green and was only able to halve the hole. Azinger won. Rumour has it that Ballesteros is still smarting from this defeat. I was amazed to read recently that Seve even went as far as accusing the upright Paul Azinger of skulduggery over this incident.

Those who score high on the Need-for-Achievement will tend to do better in competitions which take place over a long period, for instance, knockout competitions. Each victory feeds their confidence and paves the way for another victory. That is why people who win matchplays will tend to be good at matchplays, even if they do not do particularly well in other types of competitions. That is also the reason why people who had their first victories when they were young, get accustomed to the idea of winning and continue to win for a long time. In golf the psychological factors in the mind are far more important than any physical decline. There is nothing like a record of success to nourish future achievements.

The Fear-of-Failure reflects the dread of disapproval. Typically, the player is torn between the wish to escape another ordeal and the desire to prove oneself. A person does not get used to defeat. The prospect is regarded with foreboding and even dread. Repeated failures are deeply demoralising. In this predicament the instinctive reaction is to abscond. To avoid another wound to self-esteem, the player will resort to various strategies. First on the list are pleas of injury. If that fails, urgent commitments elsewhere are familiar excuses. If that fails as well, there will be a subjective attempt to change the objective criteria of success or failure. For instance, the likelihood of success will be said to be small due to extraneous circumstances that have nothing to do with the individual, like poor greens, atrocious weather or bad course design. And finally, when no excuses are left, victory itself will be devalued and a sour grapes attitude will prevail. Only when he is cornered and cannot avoid the situation, will the Fear-of-Failure victim rise to the occasion and fight hard to win.

The important point to understand is that the Need-for-Achievement goes hand in hand with the Fear-of-Failure. On the surface, these two needs appear to be mutually exclusive. One naturally assumes that those who fear failure will have only a low Need-for-Achievement, but that is not so. The two syndromes operate simultaneously, and **together** contribute to success or to failure. In any given competition, the two are present and the end result reflects the balance of power between them. The Need-for-Achievement produces positive motivation to win, while the driving force behind the Fear-of-Failure is the effort to avoid

defeat. The interaction between the Need-for-Achievement and the
Fear-of-Failure can be summarised thus:

| | | NEED-for-ACHIEVEMENT (NfA) | |
		HIGH	*LOW*
FEAR **-of-** **FAILURE** **(FoF)**	*HIGH*	H/H	H/L
	LOW	L/H	L/L

Several conclusions follow:

- H/H: Those who have both high Need-for-Achievement **and**
  high Fear-of-Failure are driven to success and will work the
  hardest to achieve it. They are vulnerable to the syndrome
  known as the **Fear-of-Success**. Often when victory is within
  their grasp, something inside them snaps and prevents them
  from winning.

- H/L: Those with high Need-for-Achievement and low Fear-
  of-Failure are the daredevil go-getters with a better than average
  chance of success. They either succeed – or fail –sensationally.

- L/H: Those with a low Need-for-Achievement and a high
  Fear-of-Failure are the whimps. They are most motivated
  when the chances of victory are either particularly good or
  particularly bad.

- L/L: Those with low Need-for-Achievement and low Fear-of-
  Failure are unflappable. Since they are largely free of attacks
  of nerves, their chances of success are better than average.

SUMMARY 2: THE *NfA* AND THE *FoF*

1. The Need-for-Achievement is inherent and relentless. It is strongest when the probability of success is exactly 50%.

2. The Need-for-Achievement and the Fear-of-Failure reflect the value the player puts on victory.

3. The value of victory is in inverse proportion to the difficulty of attaining it: the harder it is to achieve the more it will be valued, and vice versa, the easier the victory, the less it will be valued.

4. The Fear-of-Failure is powered by the dread of disapproval.

5. Fear-of-Failure sufferers are skillful dodgers of painful situations.

CONTROL

Golf is like a *fata morgana:* one moment it is there, and the next it is gone. It appears and disappears with tantalising irregularity. One never possesses this game, but even beginners are possessed by it.

- Is there a way to control the ebb and flow of one's mind?

- Is there a way to control the swings of error?

- Can one ensure that performance will continue on an even keel?

The honest answer to these questions is NO. It does not matter at all how much one knows about the technical aspects of the game, or the pitfalls ahead. Suddenly, out of the blue and without any warning something will go wrong. Sometimes the loss is temporary and the player recovers quickly. But, on occasions, it takes months of hard work to regain the equanimity and the confidence lost so inexplicably. "I'm playing really well at the moment," golfers routinely qualify their reply.

Lost concentration, buckling under pressure, tanking and quitting are frequent phenomena in important competitions. Some people thrive in tense situations, others go suddenly to pieces. Clearly, without any noticeable injury, the technical ability itself could not have suffered such a catastrophic decline in a matter of a few hours. So what happened? Whatever it is, the solution must be looked for in the mind. But as all good sleuths will tell you, knowing where to look for an answer is not the same as finding it. Both psychology and neurology have made important progress in recent years, but the mind keeps its own counsel.

Golf is full of paradoxes and none is more intriguing than the chameleon nature of control. The more one desires it, the more elusive it becomes. To execute a perfect swing one needs to pass certain critical points, but to initiate a swing with such thoughts in mind is doomed to failure. To gain control one must surrender one's will, and it must be done with joy and acceptance, not as a grudging sacrifice. Don't force it, just let it happen. It sounds easy but is, in effect, inordinately hard, because the fundamental tenet of our upbringing from the earliest age is the notion of controlling ourselves and controlling our environment. The idea that this could be achieved only by an unconditional, unilateral surrender of our will is too mind-boggling.

AROUSAL

In sport as in other activities, arousal is responsible for the mobilisation of energy in pursuit of a goal. The higher the level of arousal, the more energy is spent. Conversely when arousal is low, the organism will react lethargically. Kerr argues that arousal is a continuum, rather than an on/off switch. According to him arousal oscillates between: *anxiety, excitement, boredom,* and *relaxation.* High arousal manifests itself in either anxiety or excitement, depending on the circumstances; and low arousal is experienced as either boredom or relaxation.

In 1908 the psychologists, Yerkes and Dodson, proposed a model of behaviour which excited much interest (and in due course much criticism). The model examined the relationship between arousal and performance. The preliminary findings were as expected: The higher the arousal the better was the performance. That was hardly a shattering discovery. What made their study a landmark in sport psychology was the fact that this relationship was true only up to a certain point. This point is known as the point of optimal arousal. Any further arousal beyond this point was dysfunctional. In other words, Yerkes and Dodson demonstrated that performance deteriorates when arousal is either too low or too high. This relationship is known as the Inverted-U-Function. A typical example looks like this:

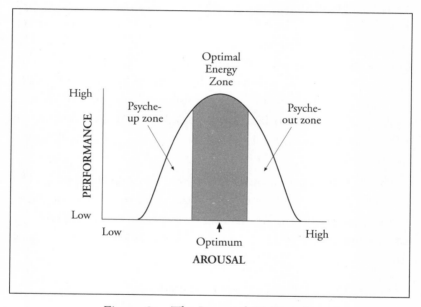

Figure 3.   The Inverted-U-Function

The shaded area is the optimal arousal zone. The two bars mark the limits beyond which performance decline. In the Psyche-up zone arousal is too low, and the player needs an energy booster. In the Psyche-out zone arousal is too high. The player is overexcited and needs calming down. The example of the Inverted-U-Function above is an idealised presentation. Any real performance will naturally be more rugged.

The validity of the Inverted-U-Function was verified by thousands of studies. In recent years, however, some sport psychologists consider the relationship 'too simple' and have suggested various improvements and elaborations. But even the most sophisticated approaches to arousal and performance, most notably, the catastrophe model of Lew Hardy, incorporate the basic premises of the Inverted-U-Function.

Over-arousal is a mental condition in which the player becomes hypersensitive to his environment. In this state, the sensory system becomes super-active and the player is bombarded by too many signals. Some of these cues are relevant to his task but others, like a gang of saboteurs, interfere and obstruct it. The golfer becomes a target at which venomous arrows are shot from all directions. The process of selecting and blocking out irrelevant signals, which is essential for optimal performance, becomes impaired, and the concentration is destroyed. The physiological symptoms of this condition are only too familiar: a pounding heart, legs turning to jelly, weak bladder, butterflies in the stomach, buckling knees, a squeaky voice.

When the level of arousal is too low, the reverse happens. The player is in a state of sensory deprivation, and the signals are either too few for good decision making or too faint to be properly registered and evaluated in the brain. The player operates in a fog of uncertainty.

There are three modes of sensory perception:

- **visual,**
- **auditory,**

   and

- **kinaesthetic.**

Some see the shot in their mind's eye, and their execution of it is a close copy of what they have already visualised. Jack Nicklaus 'goes to the movies'. He operates in the **visual** mode of perception.

I once had the good fortune of playing with a famous Irish golfer. On the fourth hole he pushed his tee shot behind a tree. The tree had a forked trunk and the ball came to rest just a few feet behind it. He glanced at the twelve-inch gap and a delighted smile curled his lips. I watched in horror as he took out his 5-wood and prepared to hit the ball through the narrow gap in the tree. Were he to miss and hit the tree, the ball would most probably ricochet sideways and, with his power, kill me. Involuntarily, I fell to my knees and crouched in fear behind my golf bag. I waited tensely but nothing happened. I peeped out cautiously and saw the rascal standing there with a broad smile on his face. "You coward!" he exclaimed with a twinkle in his eyes, and hit the ball, which flew through the narrow gap all the way to the green. "Sorry I've doubted you," I apologised still stunned. It was a virtuoso shot. "I saw it all in advance, I couldn't miss it," he explained as he calmly put the club back in the bag.

Some golfers, like Fuzzy Zoeller, talk to themselves about yardage, wind, elevation, the hardness of the ground and whatever else seems relevant to them, sounding much like a chartered surveyor. They operate in the **auditory** mode of perception. What the visual player does in silence, they have to verbalise before they can act.

Finally, there are the **kinaesthetic** golfers like Ballesteros, who feel the shot in their body. "My right index finger gives me a lot of information and a terrific feel for the putt," Seve divulged to the baffled interviewer. Most good golfers are visual and kinaesthetic. They 'see' and 'feel' the shot before they execute it.

To predict the stability of performance one needs to know how arousal changes during the competition. Unfortunately, this is one of the toughest enigmas in golf. In an ideal world, optimal arousal would remain constant throughout the round and the player will be in that heaven called 'the zone'. But in most rounds, arousal fluctuates around the optimal level.

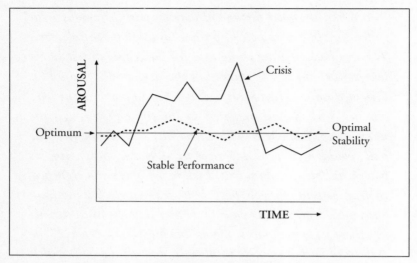

Figure 4. Stable and crisis performance

The sharper the deviations, the worse will be the performance. Golf is unforgiving. The margins of error are very small. To play five shots over the handicap is dismal, eight shots is a crisis, and to shoot anything worse than that is a catastrophe. People with a narrow Inverted-U-Function are more volatile and more vulnerable because small changes in arousal result in big changes in performance. Conversely, when the Inverted-U-Function is flat, fluctuations in arousal result in only moderate changes in performance and, therefore, less overall variation.

What exactly is optimal arousal? Every sport has its special requirements and every person his special needs. Golf is a game of precision and analysis, not of brute strength and speed. Moderate levels of arousal are best suited for stable performance. Power tasks, on the other hand, require higher levels of arousal. To box, wrestle, play tennis or soccer, the player must be pumped up. Similarly, the execution of simple mindless tasks, like hammering nails or chopping wood, benefits from higher arousal, but that of complicated cognitive tasks deteriorates.

When the player is 'cool', the mind is tuned in, and the world is tuned out. The interaction between the player, the ball and the

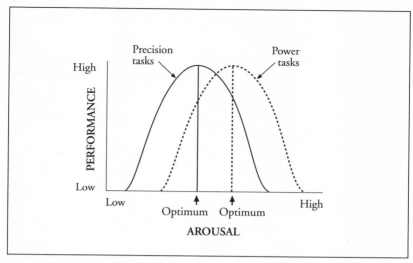

Figure 5. Optimal arousal: power and precision tasks

course is all that matters; nothing else exists. The player is cocooned inside a bubble: seeing everything, hearing everything, understanding everything, but being affected by nothing. Decision making is lucid and executed faultlessly with tension at its lowest ebb. There

In the zone...

is no hesitation or agonising, no doubt and questioning, only serene dispatch.

Extraverts require more stimulation to get going. They attain their best performances at relatively high levels of arousal. By contrast, introverts, who are 'augmenters' by nature, are psyched-up at comparatively low levels of arousal, and over-excitation tends to be counterproductive.

The age at which one is initiated into the game is very important. Those who learn to play young, while still in a state of innocence and grace, will enjoy an easier time later in their golfing life. Tiger Woods' father revealed that his son climbed out of his cot at the ripe age of ten months, reached for a golf club and swung left-handed, the mirror image of his dad. So precocious was the toddler that some months later, he spontaneously realised his mistake and began to swing right-handed. It was then that the elder Woods began to suspect that he was the begetter of a future grand master of golf.

Those who learn to play young and then abandon the game for many years, still play more consistently than those who came to the game later in life. The swing is executed without thought, just like walking, or driving, or swimming. If anyone constantly analysed the complicated series of movements, which amount to any of the 'simple' activities we normally engage in, the performance of that activity would suffer greatly. Nothing is easier than throwing a ball. But the moment one stops to think about direction and velocity, the exact position of the wrist, the grip, and the turn of the shoulder, the throw is as good as doomed. If, in addition, one uses a club instead of one's hand, it is a miracle that one succeeds at all.

Those who suffer from high trait anxiety, perform best when arousal is low. Their Inverted-U-Function is narrow and performance declines sharply when arousal increases beyond the optimal point. By contrast, unflappable players need to be more strongly aroused in order to achieve peak performance. Their Inverted-U-Function is flatter and shows steady improvement till the optimal point is reached, as well as gradual, rather than abrupt decline, once it is passed.

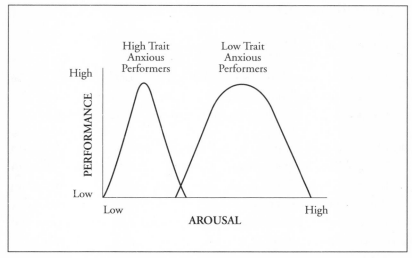

Figure 6. Optimal arousal: anxious and non-anxious players

The relationship between performance and **state anxiety** is more complex. You may recall that **state anxiety** has two elements: a cognitive rational aspect and a physiological aspect. The catastrophe model of Lew Hardy takes into account the interaction between these two elements and predicts that:

- Performance will benefit from rising levels of cognitive anxiety, if physiological arousal remains low.

- Performance will be destroyed by rising levels of cognitive anxiety, if physiological arousal is high.

- Performance will not be significantly affected by changes in physiological arousal, if the level of cognitive anxiety is low.

Golf is prone to sudden shifts in mood and arousal levels. Unlike most other ball games, speed is not of the essence and the activity consists mainly of a long stroll with a target, or rather 18 targets, in mind. It involves a high level of concentration and cognitive decision making which is best done in a calm and collected atmosphere.

SUMMARY 3: AROUSAL

1. Optimal arousal is crucial to good performance.

2. Increased arousal improves the player's performance till he reaches the optimal point. Any further increase beyond this point will be counterproductive, and will cause obstruction.

3. Optimal performance depends on the *level* of arousal and on its *stability*. Players, whose optimal arousal endures through the vicissitudes of the game (flatter Inverted-U-Function), stand a much better chance of doing well than those whose arousal is more volatile. Their performance is robust even under stress and provocation. Less stable players tend to crack up and founder.

4. Optimal arousal differs from individual to individual and from sport to sport.

5. Extraverts need more stimulation than introverts.

6. Precision sports require a low level of arousal, and power sports – a high one.

7. The only way to achieve control in golf is to relinquish the desire for it and *trust* the body to perform.

8. Performance depends on the interaction between cognitive anxiety and physiological arousal.

3: Survival Strategies

Before Nick Faldo met Ben Hogan for the first time, he is rumoured to have spent a sleepless night, thinking of all the questions he wanted to put to his great idol. He listed three pages of questions concerning technique, four pages about the psychology of the game, and three additional pages regarding winners' mentality. Evidently, Faldo was far more interested in psychological illumination than in technical know-how, though Hogan is considered to be the supremo of mechanical golf.

Mental training is an integral part of practice and ought to follow similar disciplined routines. Stress-management programmes are aimed at enabling the player to achieve his highest potential without becoming a nervous wreck in the process. They provide the necessary tools to anticipate trouble and ward it off. The most important stress-management techniques are:

- goal-setting,
- relaxation,
- stress inoculation,
- hypnosis,
- cognitive stress-management, and
- performance routines.

I shall discuss each of them in turn.

GOAL-SETTING

Lee Trevino set himself the modest goal never to leave the practice green before he chipped into a hole. Tiger Woods set his sights on dazzling the world by winning all four majors in his first year as a professional. He did not. Tom Watson practised holing from tough places. When he found himself in the rough, tied for the championship with Jack Nicklaus on the last day of the 1982 US

Open, he played **The Chip.** "Knock it close," said his caddy in one of the most famous exchanges ever recorded on the golf course. "Close?" retorted Tom, "I'm going to knock it in." And to the enthrallment of millions, he did.

Goal-setting is the determination to achieve a specific target, no matter what. It is a binding contract with oneself to accomplish certain objectives. There are two types of goals:

- **outcome goals,**
  and
- **performance goals.**

Outcome goals are the objectives that one sets out to achieve: win the club championship, beat certain opponents, reduce handicap. Performance goals specify the means of achieving these objectives.

An effective strategic plan includes both outcome and perform-ance goals. But during a competition, the emphasis must be on **performance** goals and not on outcome goals. Always focus on the information necessary for the correct shot – distance, terrain, wind, club – not on **how** to execute the shot and emphatically not on what the shot must achieve and the dire consequences if it does not achieve it. The thinking process may run something like this: *The pin is in the upper tier of the green. The green slopes from right to left. I'll aim just right of the flag and try to keep the ball below the flag.* Not: I must get a par here. Not: I must improve my eclectic score on this hole. Not: I want to win this competition. The quickest route to winning is forgetting about winning and concentrating, instead, on playing just one shot at a time.

Goals are more than simply things we want. To merit that description they must be:

- specific,

- challenging,

- realistic, and

- attainable in the foreseeable future.

To take a firm decision to do 'something', or 'work harder' is not good enough. One needs to be precise about the parameters of execution. The situation is rather like that of an overweight person who wishes to become slimmer. It is not enough to decide to lose weight. One needs to know exactly what to eat and what not to eat; how much to eat, and when not to eat at all. In other words, the targets should be well defined, simple and measurable.

Easy goals will not do. Real targets must be challenging. When goals are too easily accomplished, their value depreciates, and there is always a sneaking suspicion that they were bogus in the first place. A sense of struggle is germane to any worthwhile goal.

On the other hand, targets which are the stuff of fantasy and fanciful ambition, are as effective as daydreams. Goals must be attainable. They ought to be rooted in the stern reality of the golfer's capability and the amount of effort he is prepared to put into improving himself. Last but not least, goals are not goals if they do not have a binding timetable. Deciding to win something one day is equivalent to being invited to dinner sometime by a new acquaintance. It won't happen unless there is a deadline.

Effective goal-setting is like a ladder, where each rung is a short-term assignment that must be accomplished before the next objective can be tackled. Short-term goals are attractive because they offer immediate rewards. The most important reward is enhanced self-confidence. "Progress," says Orlick, "is a series of ups and downs." Slipping down the ladder encourages the player to think and try again. *(See Do-It-Yourself 1, p65).*

Goal-setting sets in motion three powerful mechanisms:

1. It shapes attention and action.

2. It determines the amount of effort one is prepared to invest in the task.

3. It drives people to develop new strategies when the old ones fail.

Fascinating research revealed that the harder and more specific the goal, the more accomplished will be the performance. People are trying harder when they know what they want to achieve and when they know it is difficult. They try even harder when the target was set by themselves rather than imposed by others, and when they work for a cause rather than just for self-gratification.

About a week after I had received my official handicap, I found myself in a matchplay. I did not have the foggiest idea what I was supposed to do, except that I had to hang on. When I arrived on the first tee, barely three minutes before the match was set to begin, I found my adversary on the practice green. A caddy was fussing around him, collecting the balls.

My opponent was an immaculately dressed and coiffed 18- handicapper, and he was not having a very good day. On the first hole he shot six and I shot seven. That jolted him a bit and he began to play better. Soon he found himself three up, and the smile appeared on his thin lips. He became visibly more relaxed. I was pulling my trolley up a steep hill, when he gallantly offered his help. His own trolley was pulled by the caddy, he explained. Now, it did not escape my attention that he had not offered to pull my trolley before, when he was not comfortably up. Something about the way he did it, the condescending smile and the patronising air made me furious. I declined politely.

My next drive ended in a bush perched on a hillside. Groaning inwardly I eyed the ball nestling in the middle of the shrubbery and pulled the five-iron from my bag. As I was trying to address the ball, standing precariously at an obtuse angle to the slope, another caddy happened to pass by. "No! NO!" he shook his head emphatically, though he was not asked. "No! Take a pitching wage and get out." Anyone knew what to do better than I did. I obeyed and the ball came out flying onto the edge of the green to the great displeasure of my opponent. It lay about twenty-five feet away from the hole, so there was no great danger of a par, but the putt went in. My adversary clenched his teeth and with real bile intoned: "Did anyone ever tell you that you have a dreadful putting stroke?"

I did not reply. It is true that my putting stroke is not conventional, but it works for me. I won that hole, and from that moment on never looked back. "It is my birthday today," the man told me plaintively with a dejected air as we shook hands on the eighteenth green. "My wife will be disappointed," he added with a dash of reproach. He did not cut a dignified figure in defeat. I regarded him with a mixture of irritation and mirth. Why did he try to make me feel guilty? I am ashamed to admit that, like Morales in Chorus Line, I felt nothing. Underneath it all was a warm glow of satisfaction and a sense of well-being. I won against the odds and it definitely felt good. That was my initiation into matchplay, and it has remained my forte.

Distant goals are more difficult to achieve than those which are close at hand. Reducing the handicap to single figures is considerably harder than reducing it by a shot or two. Practising one hour a day is easy in the first couple of weeks, but less so after a month.

At the beginning of a matchplay, all the options are open and the jury is out, but at dormie three, who has the advantage? On the face of it, all the pressure is on the one who is down: he must win all three holes to force a play-off. The task is both challenging and specific. The one who is up, on the other hand, only needs to halve one hole, but he has more to lose. Enters character. The high-self-esteemer will thrive when he is down and will have a distinct advantage in this situation. The low-self-esteemer will assume that he has already lost, and the next hole is a mere formality.

SUMMARY 4: GOAL-SETTING

1. Effective goal-setting includes performance goals and outcome goals.

2. The goals must be:

   • Specific and measurable,

   • Challenging but realistic,

   • Attainable in the near future,

   • Steps in a long-term plan.

3. The goals must be practised regularly and systematically.

4. Progress must be monitored and evaluated.

5. The plan must be flexible and responsive to evolving needs.

RELAXATION

Body and mind are inseparable. A change in the one triggers a change in the other. In golf, the mind is a treacherous instrument. It acts more like an **agent provocateur** than a faithful ally. Why? The reasons are not clear. One explanation is that human nerve circuits do not have automatic regulators. This means that we do not know when there is too much tension in the body. In theory tension can rise and rise till it reaches breaking point.

The voluntary muscles *(see Figure 1, p10)* are arranged in pairs and they can work only in one direction: they pull. When muscles tense up, they contract. That sends a signal to the brain to activate the corresponding opposite muscles in order to hold that part of the body in place. This **double pull** can generate formidable tension throughout the body which manifests itself in wild shots in unpredictable directions. I vividly remember the stunned silence around the 18th green during the Portuguese Open, when David Feherty's drive sailed through the air and hit with shattering force the elegant Estoril club house. By-passing conscious detection, tension rises and the golfer becomes a war zone, where:

- Too many muscles contract,

- Rigid muscles fail to release, and

- Muscles contraction is mistimed.

The result is a total lack of coordination.

To regain form, it is imperative to break this vicious muscle-mind-muscle circle. It does not matter at which end one starts: the muscles or the brain. The mission is to break the deadly circuit of stimulus-response pattern leading to or from the brain.

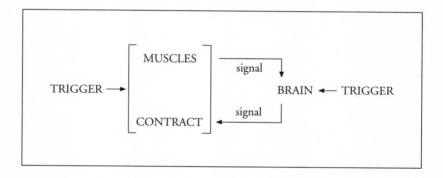

Relaxation techniques concentrate on the muscle-to-brain (**afferent**) portion of the nervous system. Their aim is to detect and release muscle tension systematically. All relaxation techniques have three objectives:

1. To induce serenity.

2. To increase awareness.

3. To prepare consciousness to receive suggestions.

Complete relaxation is a foundation skill and is the cornerstone of all body-to-mind manipulations. Like good nutrition it is not something that one does occasionally but a fundamental part of the sporting life. Since body and mind are but a mirror image of each other, many programmes combine body-to-mind and mind-to-body techniques, for instance, Yoga, meditation, autogenic training and biofeedback. Which blend is selected is to a large extent a matter of taste and personal preference.

Momentary relaxation is important just before the start of an important competition and is a godsend during trying moments in the competition itself.

The two main *muscle-to-brain* relaxation techniques are:

- **Breathing,** and
- **Progressive Muscular Relaxation.**

I. BREATHING

Breathing for relaxation is more than simply increasing the oxygen supply in the blood. It is an acquired skill, and has several forms.

1. The **deep breath** comes from the diaphragm and fills up the whole body cavity from the abdomen to the shoulders. It requires concentration and conscious effort as one first absorbs as much air as possible, and then strives to drain the lungs completely. The last bit of exhaling ejects the last bit of tension from the body. To achieve relaxation, it is necessary to take about 30 deep breaths.

To vary: take a deep breath; hold for ten seconds; exhale with a sigh.

2. **Rhythmic breathing.**

- *Carré.* This is not a poker hand but a form of breathing which involves a four-beat sequence: (Inhale/Block/Exhale /Block) each to the count of four. Repeat 20 times.
- *Carré* breathing produces a sense of balance.

- *One-to-two.* Inhale to the count of three, exhale to the count of six. There is nothing sacred about three and six. Any number will do as long as the ratio of one-to-two is kept. Repeat 20 times.
- *One-to-two* is a powerful relaxer and is excellent in inducing sleep.

- *Five-to-one.* Take a deep breath, count and visualise the number five. Exhale fully. Repeat procedure with number four. With each successive breath, tell yourself that you are more relaxed than you were during the previous breath.Repeat with numbers three, two and one.

  - *Five-to-one* is a good exercise just before competitions.

3. **Concentration breathing.** Take a deep breath while concentrating on just one thought: *"I can do it; I am going to win,"* as Sally Gunnell kept telling herself on the memorable occasion of winning the World Championship. If the mind wanders, make sure that it returns to the thought. This is a good exercise in self-discipline and is the basis of meditation.

II. PROGRESSIVE MUSCULAR RELAXATION (PMR)

The second muscle-to-brain master technique is Progressive Muscular Relaxation.

- The **Basic Progressive Muscular Relaxation** technique involves tensing and relaxing in turn all the muscle groups in the body. *(For detailed workout, see Do-It-Yourself 2, p66).*

- The great disadvantage of Progressive Muscular Relaxation is that it takes too long. Once mastered, however, an **abbreviated** procedure can be used. This involves the tensing and relaxing of major muscle **groups** rather than individual muscles in turn.

- In the extreme and in extremity, tense all muscle groups together, 'HOLD' for ten seconds, and release. This **'quick-fix'** is very useful during trying times on the course. It channels all the anger, frustration and aggression into the tensing up while the release provides, at least, some relief.

III. PASSIVE PROGRESSIVE RELAXATION

This procedure follows the same steps as Progressive Muscular Relaxation but it omits the tensing part. In other words, the technique concentrates on **release** only.

IV. DIFFERENTIAL RELAXATION

Pause and listen to your body. Are any of your muscles tense? Which muscles are tense and which are not? How tense are they? To enable you to answer these questions, use differential relaxation. This technique teaches muscle awareness.

The procedure has three stages. In the first stage one contracts the major muscle groups in turn. In the second stage one contracts the muscles only half as much as in the first stage. Finally one generates just enough tension to carry out the task. This technique teaches awareness of the participating muscles and how to detect excess tension.

V. QUICK BODY SCAN

The quick body scan looks for spots of tension. It can be carried out at any time. The neck and shoulders are particularly vulnerable and should be checked regularly.

SUMMARY 5: RELAXATION

1. Relaxation techniques are aimed at controlling the mind through controlling the muscles. There are two foundation skills: **breathing** and **progressive muscular relaxation.**

2. The main breathing techniques are:
   - **the deep breath,**
   - *carré,*
   - **one-to-two,** and
   - **five-to-one.**

3. Concentration breathing is deep breathing while focusing on one thought.

4. Progressive muscular relaxation is a **tense/release** procedure of the major muscle groups.

5. Differential relaxation focuses on distinguishing and recognising degrees of tension in the muscles.

6. Passive progressive relaxation concentrates on **RELEASE** only.

7. Quick body scan pays particular attention to tension in the neck and shoulders.

STRESS INOCULATION

Stress inoculation, or desensitisation as it is otherwise known, was invented by Meichenbaum. The idea is quite simple and is taken from preventive medicine. It consists of an injection of a weak dose of the disease – stress here. This encourages the mind to develop 'antibodies' to it so that, when the disease attacks in full force, the person is ready to defend himself. In golf, the scales are heavily tipped in favour of an attack of nerves, and the more mentally prepared one is, the better are the chances of survival.

Stress Inoculation involves three phases:

- education,
- rehearsal, and
- application.

The **educational phase** exposes the players to their own thoughts and feelings during stressful experiences. It is a process of self-enlightenment: Knowledge is power, and self-knowledge is absolute power. It works by:

- Breaking stress into manageable units, and
- By identifying the particular stressors which bother the player most.

During the **rehearsal phase,** the player learns to recognise the warning signals and the means to ward them off. These cover three important areas:

1. **Analytical appraisal** of the situation and assessment of possible solutions. As long as the player is capable of cool analysis and does not panic, he is in command of his emotions and able to take decisions and act on them.

2. **Physiological approach:** This includes an array of relaxation techniques, aimed at controlling and reducing arousal by utilising muscle-to-mind methods, e.g. breathing, Yoga, stretching, physiotherapy.

3. **Mental approach:** Mind-to-muscle methods. The ousting of destructive thoughts by the conscious imposition of positive self-statement is called cognitive restructuring. This is not mumbo-jumbo but a proven way of altering negative states of mind. For a discussion of various mental techniques, see sections below.

The typical desensitisation training progresses in stages. First, the player relaxes, using one of the available techniques, like progressive muscular relaxation or Yoga. For example, he might be asked to lie flat on his back, close his eyes, and begin a detailed survey of his body, relaxing each part as he goes along. The survey begins with the head and ends with the toes. It takes about ten minutes. At the end of this procedure, the body is rag-like and totally limp and the mind is ready to receive suggestions.

In the second stage, the psychologist introduces one of the tormenting stressors. The player must remain calm while imagining himself playing with the stressor present. The training continues till the player manages to function smoothly in spite of the disturbing interference. When one stressor is mastered in that way, the training moves on to the next problem on the list, and so on till, in an ideal world, the desensitisation process is complete.

The **application phase** places the player in a mildly threatening situation. Once he learns to cope, the threat increases till it reaches levels similar to those in a real competition. Naturally, make-belief stress is less painful than the real thing. To drive the lessons home, a number of training programmes simulate highly perturbing, realistic, embarrassing and even alarming situations. A lot depends on the trainers' fertile – some claim sadistic – minds. For instance, the subject might be abandoned in a maze to find his way out to safety; or he might be exposed to unsettling and sometimes terrifying images, reminiscent of those in *Back To The Future* in Universal Studios, Hollywood. For those who go all out for punishment, the imaginary terrors are replaced with something more mundane, but arguably more potent, ie an electrical shock. Yes, to improve themselves, some people do go to extremes.

Of course, it is impossible to foresee every predicament. One day, when I lived in Portugal, my husband was approached by a young man.

"May I have your permission to play with your wife in the next mixed pairs knockout competition?" he asked rather formally. "If you wish, and she agrees," my husband gave his consent none too enthusiastically. The young man had a weakness for older women.

I arrived for the first match ready to do justice to Pedro's confidence in me. I ought perhaps to mention that Pedro was a good fifteen years younger than myself and of Latin appeal. He greeted me on the tee by kissing my hand. Portugal is old-fashioned, but Pedro was ceremonious even by Portuguese standards.

"Please meet Maria Theresa," he then said, indicating his girl friend. She was a charming lady with a mass of curly white hair, falling down to her shoulders, and she was in her mid-fifties.

We shook hands. Maria Theresa smiled at me bashfully and clutched Pedro's arm possessively. I realised with dismay that she meant to accompany us on the course. A couple of curious onlookers stopped to watch Pedro teeing off.

"Superb shhhot," Maria Theresa intoned breathlessly.

My drive ended in a ditch. She smiled at me without any malice and threw a quick look at Pedro as though to make sure that all was well. I managed a par on the second hole and Pedro gave me the thumbs up. As I walked away from the green, I caught a look on Maria Theresa's face which stopped me in my tracks. She had large dark eyes and they were full of fear and pain.

"Bother!" I muttered to myself as the realisation dawned upon me that she did not want me to play well. It was like emotional blackmail. Maria-Theresa was beseeching me to understand that her very happiness, maybe even life, was at stake. Pedro was her love, her joy, her raison d'être. Nothing should happen to make him notice, let alone like anyone else. "I am married," I wanted to tell her. "I am not into young men. Don't worry!" But it was useless. She was frantic and I was under surveillance. As though on cue, I started to play badly. There was nothing I could do about it. I could not wait for the match to end, and when we lost, I humbly apologised to Pedro for my appalling play.

"You had a bad day," he had his own explanation. I looked at him curiously. How could he be so blind? Did he really believe that? Perhaps it was the truth?

The chief reason that experienced players are better at stress management than novices is precisely the knowledge they have accumulated and the inbuilt defence they have developed over the years. What is this defence? It has been noted before that anxiety has two aspects: cognitive (= worry), and emotional (= somatic/physiological). Each has its own cures.

Worry can be tackled effectively by cognitive restructuring techniques, which are designed to eradicate negative thinking and improve poor self-image. Performance is enhanced by creating positive expectations, by eliminating distracting and destructive thoughts and by preventing self-rumination. Some techniques commonly used are: meditation, self-talk, imagery, goal-setting and hypnosis.

Somatic anxiety can be lowered by physical exercise, physio-therapy, Yoga, biofeedback and autogenic training.

Some of these techniques are discussed in this book. Along with regular practice, many good golfers and most international players make use of at least some aspects of mental training programmes.

SUMMARY 6: STRESS INOCULATION

Stress inoculation involves three stages:

1. Self enlightenment about the major sources of stress.
2. Rehearsal, which include early recognition of warning signals, and an array of physical and mental techniques to keep stress under control.
3. Application of stressors in ever increasing doses till the golfer becomes immune to their effect.

HYPNOSIS

Hypnosis has been employed as a therapeutical technique for over a hundred years. Contrary to popular belief, Freud did not invent hypnosis; he only used it to prove his theory of the unconscious. The argument is that if a player of a known ability suffers, for no apparent reason, a relapse in his performance, he must be hampered by something in his mind. Hypnosis relieves stress by:

- Providing an outlet for bottled-up emotions.
- Releasing energy which has been tied up in internal turmoil.
- Focusing attention.
- Helping to master anxiety, anger and emotionality.
- Contributing to higher motivation, self-efficacy and enthusiasm.

Weinberg has conducted a series of fascinating studies on the use of hypnotic suggestion. He gave his subjects a set of positive instructions under hypnosis about a task that they were about to tackle.

Their performance was 30% better than normal when they were in a hypnotic state, and 25% better than normal when they were in a post-hypnotic state. On the other hand, when he gave them a set of negative instructions under hypnosis, their performance dropped a sharp 25%.

"What do you feel?" the psychologist asked the athletic look-ing young man, who was lying on the sofa in a hypnotic trance.

"I feel as though my hands are tied with a rope and I can't swim," said the man wistfully. He was a water polo player in his country's national team.

The psychologist had an idea. He got up and went to his desk. From a drawer he took out a sharp knife. "I'll tell you what I'm going to do to help you. I'm holding a sharp knife in my hand, and with this knife I'm going to cut the rope which ties your hands. Give me your hands."

The patient extended his hands, holding them clasped together as though they were bound. The psychologist examined the 'knot', making sure the subject could feel his touch. Then he cut the 'knot' slowly and very deliberately.

"I've cut the rope and your hands are free," he announced when he had finished. "You can swim now and nothing can stop you."

This is a true story, one among many. The patient thus liber-ated from his shackles, resumed his career with great success.

In spite of the hype surrounding hypnosis, there is nothing mystical about it. It is a procedure like any other procedure. The rate of success depends on how resistant people are to being put into a trance, and how receptive they are to suggestions. Contrary to popular belief, one does not lose all control under hypnosis. During the hypnotic trance the subject is questioned about his difficulties.

Being hypnotised means that he will, subject to certain limitations, reveal his innermost thoughts and feelings. That, in an ideal world, would enable the hypnotist to unlock the particular complex that arrests his performance and set him free to achieve his full potential. The problem is that things are not that simple, and even if they were, not everyone is keen on chancing the good ministrations of the hypnotist. After all, it is impossible to know what obnoxious secrets may be revealed while under hypnosis, or what solutions the hypnotist might suggest. The second and far more pertinent difficulty is that anxiety is a recurring malaise and cannot be cured once and for all. Hypnosis may work for a while, but like any other tranquilliser, it will need to be 'topped up'. There is a grave risk of becoming dependent upon the hypnotist and unable to function at all without the help of hypnosis.

Self-hypnosis is a halfway solution. Because it is self-administered, it does not quite have all the credentials of proper hypnosis. Like sexual self-indulgence, it releases tension, but is not quite the real thing. The procedure typically begins with a focusing device and progressive relaxation. It is followed by a prerecorded tape, which is designed to boost confidence. If self-hypnosis does not help, it does not do any harm either. *(See Do-It-Yourself 3, p67).*

COGNITIVE STRESS MANAGEMENT

Stress is not triggered by a given situation but by one's perception of it. It is all in the mind. If the player believes that the onlookers are mocking his peculiar swing, the chances are that he will become self-conscious, and his game will suffer. In fact, they might be laughing at a joke. Even if they were laughing at his swing, the response to ridicule is a matter of personality. Eamon D'Arcy, Raymond Floyd and Jim Furyk frankly could not care less. Others may be more sensitive. Gamesmanship exploits the opponents' weaknesses. "You swing like an Apache!" declared a friendly adversary, referring to the flourish in which the player brandished the

Critical others...

club at the top of the back swing. It was enough to ruin his game.
Stress is caused when a player:

- Perceives himself threatened by defeat or humiliation, what the Japanese describe with trepidation as a 'loss of face'.
- Fears that his coping resources are not good enough to grapple with the threat.
- Fears ruinous consequences to himself, resulting from his useless efforts to defend oneself.

According to Carver, the player in a stressful situation has three options:

1. When he reckons that he could do something to remove the threat, he will resort to **problem-solving** strategies:

   - Information gathering,
   - Action plan,
   - Targeting best response, and
   - Getting instrumental help.

Sometimes the process takes time. On other occasions, it is not uncommon to overhear a golfer muttering to himself: "I've just realised what I'm doing wrong," before he goes on to play like a pro.

2. When the player knows that he can do nothing to get rid of the threat, he will resort to **emotion-focused** strategies, whose primary aim is to help him to tolerate the stress:

- Seeking emotional support,
- Positive re-interpretation of stressful events,
- Acceptance of the situation,
- Denial of the situation,
  and even
- Turning to religion.

3. When the player does not know what to do, he will **disengage** physically and mentally from the distressing situation. In essence, he opts for a non-coping strategy. Instead of confronting the problem, he finds refuge in:

- Wishful thinking,
- Cursing the opponent and giving him the evil eye,
- Self-pity, and
- Self-blame.

Stress management employs **mind-to-muscle (efferent)** procedures. Unlike relaxation which starts from the muscles and seeks to calm the brain, these techniques start with a deliberate mind action and seek to calm the muscles. The most popular mind-to-muscle techniques will be discussed in turn:

- imagery,
- self-talk,
- simulation, and
- attention control.

IMAGERY

A recent survey revealed that imagery is extremely widespread among athletes, and is used by well over 90% of them. It is the single most popular mind controlling technique in sport. Imagery is good but some images are better than others. The more vivid and lifelike they are, the better they work. Although images are 'only' deliberately conjured hallucinations, they are amazingly effective. They work by creating an experience in the mind and in the muscles which is very similar to a real happening. Therefore, the body can learn from it in much the same way that it learns from practice.

One of the great advantages of imagery is its enormous versatility. It is an important form of practice and is absolutely vital during the game. Indeed, the best practice is one that combines imagery with action. If a golfer cannot practise for some reason, imagery is a very good substitute and certainly better than no practice at all. There are several types of imagery:

- A snap shot,

- A film sequence,

- A view from outside: watching oneself as though on television,

- A view from inside: experiencing how it feels when playing certain shots.

The video of the mind can be manipulated in various ways. It can be ordered to:

1. Screen confidence-boosting episodes from one's past.

2. Replay on demand a celebrity parade of the best and famous. There is nothing quite so inspiring as memorable golf shots.

3. Create new experiences *à la carte.*

4. Practise different shots, using as many variants as desired without fear of embarrassment or humiliation.

5. Pose and solve problems.

On the course, imagery is an indispensable weapon. Oscar Wilde, in a famous reply, told the US Customs that he had nothing to declare except his genius. There is no top golfer in the world who is not proficient in the art of conjuring images. Ordinary club players would find their game much improved if they stopped to visualise the shot before they executed it. It is absolutely essential when it comes to putting. If you believe and have the courage to wait, the true line from the ball to the hole will materialise on the green, as though drawn by a magic pencil. *(See Do-It-Yourself 4, p68).*

SELF-TALK

Cognitive restructuring is about turning the tables on negative thoughts. Instead of thinking: I have no length; think: I am accurate. Instead of telling yourself: I am going to pieces; tell yourself: I've been in worse spots before and I've come through. There's still time. I can do it.

Do not accept the harsh judgement of the prosecutor in your mind. Argue, instead, the case for the defence. You are in the court of self-belief and you can call any evidence and all the witnesses

The courtroom of the mind …

you want. You may protest and reasonably object that telling your-self flattering things is bogus and is not going to work. Remember, though, that it is **you** who thinks the bad thoughts about yourself, and that they are not any truer than the good thoughts just because they are negative. It is back to the business of the self-destructive power of the mind. No one can do a better demolishing job on our self-confidence than we can, and do. It is a strange fact that, though we are selfish and love ourselves dearly, we are con-siderably less successful in building ourselves up than in putting ourselves down.

The functions of self-talk are to:

• Recognise problems and weaknesses and put them in perspective.

• Boost confidence by reminding oneself of good performances and past glories.

• Seek advice.

• Identify the best swing thought.

• Act as a quick-fix device on the course.

The best swing thought is something like the mantra in meditation. It is a trigger which reminds the mind and the muscles to behave. Effective swing thoughts have the same two-beat movement as a golf swing: TEM-PO; LET-GO; OM-PAHH; F-OFF.

Self-talk can be used to enter a dialogue with great experts. Would you like to have Faldo's advice? Or your pro's? Or David Leadbetter's? Or even Freud's? You can call them up for an imaginary chat.

If things go wrong on the course, self-talk can be used for a quick-fix. When the urge to call yourself an idiot is overwhelming, tense instead all your muscles and say: (STOP! – SWITCH!) Take an empowering breath, exhale all tension, close your eyes, refocus and play. Remind yourself to switch channels: Snap your fingers and say: (STOP! – PLAY!). Sam Snead used (COOL – MAD). For John Daly, one word suffices: KILL!

Some people find it useful to make their own 'mastery and coping' tape, which extols their virtues and lists their achievements. They listen to it several times a day.

SIMULATION

Simulation is a mental preview of a situation. Mae West said of herself that when she was good, she was very good, but when she was bad she was better. The same is true with simulation: it is useful when it enacts 'normal' conditions, but it is invaluable when it prepares one to deal with really scary scenarios. One can never be too-ready for a tough competition. *(See Do-It-Yourself 5, p69)*.

There are three forms of simulation:

- rehearsal,

- emulation, and

- role playing.

Simulating disastrous scenarios is designed to make the real thing seems easy by comparison. For best results, carry out your simulation at the scene of the crime: on the course. Practise coping with:

- Distractions of all kinds,

- Crippling anxiety,

- Negative thinking, and

- Extreme conditions (eg bad weather).

Many amateurs have remarked on the uncanny fact that merely watching perfection has the power to improve the swing. I once saw in *The Times* a picture of Sam Torrance chipping. The ball was well on its way to the green but Sam was still looking down. I understood for the first time what it means to keep the head still. Finally, pretending to be Mr Perfect and behaving as he would have done, can have a liberating effect on the individual. After all, Mr Perfect is unlikely to make the mistakes of yours truly.

In summary, stress management teaches the player two things:

1. On the physical side, how to use relaxation techniques to control over-arousal.

2. On the mental side, how to eliminate destructive thoughts and bring about a positive frame of mind.

With sufficient training the player can achieve an altered mental state within seconds. This is a precious asset in tough situations and may make all the difference between winning and losing.

ATTENTION CONTROL

In golf, concentration is the name of the game, and it is hard to achieve. Concentration is a heightened state of awareness that zooms in on the essential and ignores everything else. It is ***doing,*** not thinking. Like a beam of light it focuses on one thing. Someone who concentrates is ***alert and relaxed*** at the same time. The key elements of concentration are:

- A passive state of mind.

- Focusing on the task without forcing attention and, at the same time, not trying in any active sense to avoid distractions.

- Appropriate centring.

The **centre of mass** is the 'middle' point of the body. In normal conditions the weight of the body is equally distributed half above the centre of mass and half below it.

In aggressive sports the centre of mass is higher than the middle point, and in cool sports like golf it is lower. When one is properly centred, the centre of mass is in the optimal position to do battle. Anxiety and tension tend to interfere with the correct centring and lift it up. To focus on the task in hand the centre of mass must be in the right place.

On what should one focus? As a matter of principle it is best to concentrate on those aspects over which one has a measure of control.

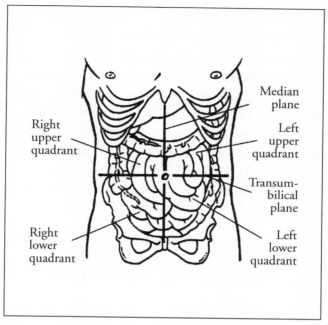

Figure 7. The Centre of Mass

Home-in on the task and task-relevant cues. FORGET the results, worries or hazards, and IGNORE the opponent.

According to Nideffer, attention has two dimensions:

- **Width:** narrow or broad focus.

- **Direction:** external or internal focus.

Width depends on the amount of information necessary to accomplish a task. In golf, there are only a few parameters to consider: i.e. the position of the ball, the distance, the direction of flight, the wind and the terrain. It is a far cry from the fast-moving scene on a football pitch.

If the cues come from the environment, the direction is said to be external. If, on the other hand, they depend on inner dialogue and feel, the direction is said to be internal. In golf, the attention style is **narrow external** with regard to shots, and **narrow internal** with regard to putting. *(See Do-It-Yourself 6, p70).*

Several studies revealed that women use inner dialogue more successfully than men do. They are also better at setting personal goals, at practising on their own and, generally, benefit more from the application of mental techniques to their game. Men are macho and fear ridicule. They prefer hard plain practice. To the annoyance of Women's Lib, Nideffer found that men are better both at attending to many stimuli at once and at concentrating on the relevant few. They also have a better internal focus than women.

PERFORMANCE ROUTINES

The previous sections dealt with various strategies which teach the player how to prepare for and deal with potential problems. Performance routines concentrate on the competition itself. How should the player compose himself just before an important competition? How should he conduct himself during the competition?

Golfers have numerous idiosyncrasies. They walk around a putt like a caged animal. They lift the putter to their nose, close one eye and look intently at the hole. They squat and cup their hands around their heads like blinkers, the better to see the line. They take practice swings, cock their eyes, stretch their shoulders and waggle the club.

Crews and Boutcher studied the behaviour of professional women golfers during a tournament. They discovered remarkable consistencies in pre-putt and pre-shot conduct. Over several hours of play these professional ladies repeatedly took the same time, the same number of practice swings and threw the same number of glances at the target, before playing each shot. All the players paid far more attention to the putts than to the long shots. Crews and Boutcher concluded that performance routines contribute physically **and psychologically** to the accuracy of the shots. They work like aide-memoires by:

- **Focusing attention** on the task in hand.
- Providing essential **warming-up** element in the interrupted flow of the game.
- Facilitating **automatic swinging.**

Good performance requires intense concentration. Once during the British Open, Faldo putted while smoke was drifting onto the green and stinging his eyes. When he raised his head, his eyes were full of tears. He was not even aware of them. Lapses in concentration allow irrelevant information to creep in and distract attention from the essential. Self-consciousness is the noose that strangles many a good golfer. Concerns over one's looks and one's swing, thoughts about the others' alleged superiority, the feeling that everyone expects one to lose – or win – the aftermath of a sleepless night and the fury at one's whimpishness wrangle in the golfer's mind like a pack of hyenas, and prevent him from applying himself to the job of playing. With single-minded determination the enemy within frustrates any attempt to regain serenity. Women, in particular, are notoriously self-conscious about the impression they make, and are far more sensitive to the 'audience effect' than are men. The mere presence of onlookers affects performance because it causes arousal.

The stop-go nature of golf means that the game starts anew after each lull. If the natural flow of the game is interrupted by waiting, or by a prolonged search for a lost ball, the chances of a wayward shot are high. Why? The player undoubtedly has not forgotten how to play in the short time that elapsed from the last shot. What happens, rather, is a temporary loss of the internal state that underlies the skill to be performed. The maintenance of this fragile equilibrium is essential for a consistent performance. The practice swing, or any other routine, helps to preserve that most precious quality known as **rhythm,** and to put the player back on track.

The ability to reestablish the internal psychological 'sets' are never as vital as when the player struggles to recover from a bad shot. Performance routines are an integral part of any shot, but after a poor shot, they perform no fewer than four vital functions. These are:

1. Post-performance analysis.
2. Rehearsal of the correct action.
3. Coping strategy.
4. Mind-clearing device.

A practice putt after a bad putt helps to exorcise the demons of uncertainty. Too many players rule themselves out of a competition after a couple of bad holes. Performance routines provide a chance of rehabilitation and create what is somewhat grandly known as affective catharsis. This is "a purification of the emotions that brings about spiritual renewal and release from tension."

Every golf shot involves analysis of distance, terrain and wind, and selection of a club. It calls for a mental picture of the ball in flight, the right feel, a good execution, an intense concentration and a silent prayer. Performance routines are essential to the maintenance of optimal physiological and psychological states during a competition. They provide the vital framework for automatic swinging, and they also play a vital role in establishing the correct mental disposition even before the first shot is played.

All the research carried out to date shows that high level of arousal is bad for golf. Low arousal and quiet determination rather than excited anticipation and thirst for blood are the correct mental attitudes. How does one achieve it? Predominantly through relaxation techniques, positive thinking and mental imagery. Once out on the golf course, it is best not to think at all. Put yourself on automatic pilot and let the cerebellum take over. If you absolutely must think, adopt just one good swing thought. "Take time to smell the flowers!"

Every player has his own optimal pace. That is the one which allows him to go through the mental and physical routines he needs. Any hurrying or slowing will dent the results. It is said of Jack

Nicklaus that he never played a shot before he was ready, and his record shows it. But to play at one's pace is not as easy as it sounds. It takes, in fact, enormous willpower to do so. The ordinary club player is under great pressure to play at the pace dictated by others, including the opponent and the group pressing from behind.

No one can fail to admire the manifest elegance, the suave ease, the economic simplicity, the poetic fluidity of the professional golfer. There is no effort, no tension, no flailing and plunging about, which is so characteristic of the club player. Behind the beautiful swing of the professional golfer are countless hours of practice. This exceedingly hard work is aimed at achieving in due course, the automatic fluidity of a thoughtless swing; when the swing becomes as reflexive and natural as the batting of an eyelid or a skip in the park.

In important competitions, when the golfer is especially keen to play really well, the calamitous tendency to attempt to control the swing by conscious thinking: "I must do this or that," creeps in. It is as though the player puts himself under surveillance and monitors his performance.

Under self-surveillance ...

Consciousness, unfortunately, is the worst guide for a fluid swing. Far from improving matters, it becomes an asphyxiating obstacle, akin to having the headmaster breathing down your neck during an exam. The mind cannot **consciously** orchestrate about 200 muscles attempting to execute one perfect swing. All motor activity, once learnt, is best left to itself. Any attempt to consciously instruct one's legs how to walk is bound to end in a fall. The mind has numerous functions to attend to. When it masters an action, it delegates it to muscle memory. The activity is put on auto-pilot which is monitored without conscious interference from a centre in the mind called the cerebellum. Any attempt to tamper with the proceedings can only result in failure. Even musicians, who have far more complicated things to do with their fingers than swing a golf club, let the fingers do the job, once they have rehearsed the piece and know it well.

SUMMARY 7: PERFORMANCE ROUTINES

1. Performance routines are especially important during competitions. They focus attention on the task, provide essential warming-up element in the interrupted flow of the game, and facilitate automatic swinging.

2. After a bad shot, they act to rehabilitate the player by analysing the mistake, rehearsing the correct action, allowing a little time for regrouping and by readying the mind for a new vigorous action.

3. To be effective, performance routines should be employed regularly in practice and in competition.

DO-IT-YOURSELF 1:
GOAL-SETTING

1. Goal: reduce handicap by x shots.

2. Set a deadline.

3. Identify the best means to achieve the goal:
   - improved length?
   - improved chipping?
   - improved putting?
   - improved mental attitude?

4. Make a detailed plan:
   - What to practise: Long game? Short game? Which woods and irons?
   - How much time/effort to devote to each aspect?
   - Set attainable sub-goals, eg chip in, be within 10" of the hole.
   - Record your results.
   - Chart your progress.
   - Be flexible: introduce modifications, if necessary.

5. Aim to win certain competitions. It provides a focus for your work, even if you don't win them.

6. Practise mental training:
   Set times: 5-15 minutes in the mornings and evenings.
   Include: relaxation, imagery, self-talk.

7. P&P: Practise and persevere. Be regular, systematic and persistent.

DO-IT-YOURSELF 2:
PROGRESSIVE MUSCULAR RELAXATION

1. Lie on your back, arms beside you, palms up.

2. Close your eyes.

3. Take several deep breaths.

4. Make a tight right hand fist and think 'HOLD'. Hold for six seconds. Think 'OK', release for 12 seconds. Repeat once.

5. Repeat procedure in the following order:

   (a) fist and upper right arm

   (b) fist and upper left arm

   (c) teeth and eyes

   (d) neck

   (e) shoulders

   (f) abdomen

   (g) buttocks

   (h) right leg: thigh, ankle, foot

   (i) left leg: thigh, ankle, foot.

6. Relax all your muscles. Scan the body for residual tension. Let it go. You would feel calm, drowsy and limp. Take a moment to enjoy it.

7. Take an empowering breath. Stretch your arms and legs. Feel the energy flowing back. Open your eyes.

For an abbreviated Progressive Muscular Relaxation:

1. Tense both arms. 'HOLD' for five seconds. 'RELEASE' for 10 seconds. Repeat once.

2. Continue with: face, shoulders, buttocks, both legs, repeating the same HOLD/RELEASE sequence as in 1.

DO-IT-YOURSELF 3: SELF-HYPNOSIS

1. Preparation: Find a quiet, comfortable room with subdued light. Make sure you will not be disturbed. Put a golf ball with a black dot painted on it on a table in front of you. Place it 30cm away from you and a little above the eyes. Have your pre-recorded message handy.

2. Sit down in front of the table, facing a blank wall with the light coming from behind. Fix your attention on the ball. Examine it minutely: its colour, shape, dimples.

3. Scan your body from head to toes. Take a deep breath. Hold it, and exhale. Tell yourself: RELAX! RELAX! RELAX! Repeat seven times. Feel your body become limper each time. Your eyes will begin to blink or water. They will get heavy till you can hardly keep them open. This is the sign that you have reached the receptive state of self-hypnosis.

4. Think into your toes. Scan them like an ultra sound. Command them to: RELAX! RELAX! RELAX! Repeat with feet, calves, thighs, buttocks, abdomen, lower back, chest, upper back, shoulders, neck, face, arms and end with the fingers.

    Close your eyes. Repeat the procedure three times. You can skip some body parts but make sure you scan the main ones.

5. Play your pre-recorded tape. It should be short, positive and powerful. Address your weaknesses boldly and honestly. For instance:

    I am a very good golfer. I have everything it takes to play well. I have complete control over my feelings, emotions and reactions. My brain is in command. It will not let me down. If I feel tense, if I have a bad shot, I will simply tell myself: RELAX! RELAX! RELAX! and the jitters will go away.

    Repeat the script several times till it becomes deeply embedded in your subconscious.

Give yourself post-hypnotic cues. For instance, when you address the ball, visualise the black dot. Feel sure that you are going to hit the ball square on the dot.

6. Before waking up, say to yourself: "When I count five I will wake up, and when I wake up, I will feel great, I will feel confident, I will feel better and play better than I have ever done before."

7. Count one, two, three, four, five and wake up feeling great.

DO-IT YOURSELF 4: IMAGERY

1. Lie down flat on your back, arms limp, palms up.

2. Close your eyes.

3. Inhale to the count of three, exhale to the count of six. Repeat seven times.

4. Think of the letter **A**. Try hard to visualise it.

5. Think of the letter **B**. Try hard to visualise it.

6. Think of the letter **C**. Try hard to visualise it.

7. See yourself on the first tee. Get absorbed in the details.
    - What is the weather?
    - What are you wearing?
    - Are you in a good mood?
    - Address the ball.
    - See your target.
    - See the ball hitting the target.
    - Watch yourself swinging the club and hitting a perfect shot.
    - Continue to 'play'.

8. Practise special shots:

    (a) bunker: ball is up-slope, down slope, buried.

    (b) chip over: a bunker, a tree, a pond.

    (c) go round corners.

9. Go to problem holes. Play them. Pay special attention to the foundering shot. Find out what needs to be done.

10. Vary the circumstances. Imagine:

    (a) Dreadful weather and yourself impervious to it.

    (b) Banter/noise and yourself impervious to it.

    (c) Playing against adversarial people. Cocoon yourself: they do not exist.

DO-IT-YOURSELF 5: SIMULATION

Start with a few deep breaths. Imagine yourself on the course. Run through the event in your mind.

1. When the weather is bad.

2. When you are nervous and jittery.

3. After a sleepless night.

4. When you are hungry and thirsty.

5. When your feet are swollen.

6. With hostile opponents.

7. Furious/hurt by unfair rulings.

8. Watched by unfriendly gallery.

9. Handling devious practices.

Cope with these aggravations, assess them coolly and emerge stronger and ready to face them.

Experiment. Repeat the scenario with a role model in the title part. Does he cope better? How does he do it?

DO-IT-YOURSELF 6: CONCENTRATION

1. How long can you concentrate on one thought? Estimate. Pick a thought. Verify.

2. How long can you look at one object before your attention begins to wander? Try looking at the moon, while thinking just one thought. Estimate, then check.

3. Use the grid concentration exercise devised by Harris and Harris *(in J M Williams, Applied Sport Psychology, p. 270)*. This is a ten-by-ten grid. Each box contains one number between 00 and 100. The numbers are scattered at random. The task is to put a slash through each number in the proper sequence. According to Harris and Harris, if you are focused, you should be able to score 20 to 30 numbers in one minute. Make the task harder by introducing noise, music, chatting. Mark your score per minute.

4. Video games are excellent focusing exercises.

5. Draw a circle. Place the tip of your pencil some distance away, close your eyes and draw a straight line to the heart of the 'green'. (Suggested by Tim Gallwey in *The Inner Game of Golf*).

6. To understand what it means to focus on something, think of taking a photo. The same sequence of events apply to a golf shot: getting ready, zooming-in, shot.

4: Practice

"It's a funny thing, the more I practise, the luckier I get."
(Gary Player)

The purpose of practice is threefold:

- To learn a new skill,
- To rehearse an acquired skill, and
- To embed the correct models of performance upon the mind.

Muscle memory is about the interaction between a mental image of perfection and its execution. *The more automatic the swing and the less conscious thinking interferes with the shot, the better will the result be.* Performance depends on confidence, and practice is a necessary but not a sufficient condition to achieve it. All it promises is that in the fullness of time the game will improve. Meanwhile, it guarantees nothing. No one knows how one will play at any given moment. All one can do is search for ways of reducing the uncertainty. You may practise till your hands are as rough as the skin of an old hog. You may have the most satisfying practice with magical shots that take your breath away and, yet, on the course, in a competition, the game evaporates into thin air like dew on a hot Summer day.

Can one control the game better? Leadbetter, the number one coach, as he modestly describes himself, believes that this can be achieved by developing a totally reliable swing. The theory is that with hard work, discipline and willpower such a swing will not collapse under pressure. The trouble is: it does. Sandy Lyle has never fully recovered his form, though he tried every remedy known to man. In the 1990 Masters, Raymond Floyd, a man well weathered in golf storms and not known for lack of courage or resolution, was stalked like a doomed animal by Nick Faldo, the champ who never gives up. And Nick himself, the defending champion, missed the cut in Augusta, when he was outclassed by the "new sheriff in town", Tiger Woods, playing in his first Masters as a pro, and shooting six under par over the last nine holes.

Practice works by transforming complex shots into simple ones. Just as actors rehearse a part till it becomes part of themselves, so does practice teach the mind and the muscles their assigned roles. The more one practises the more automatic the shots become. Naturally the simpler the shot is, the easier it would be to execute it under pressure. On seeing a ball plugged in the face of a steep bunker, a shot that most of us would have considered daunting, Lee Westwood calmly opined that it was not very difficult to get it out. One only needs to... A professional can accomplish such remarkable feats because all his shots are well rehearsed. Many shots – bunker, rough, downhill, deliberate draws and fades – are very difficult for the inexperienced golfer. The professional golfer knows what to do because the models of the correct shots are imprinted upon his mind and become, as it were, second nature. It does not follow that he will not make any mistakes, only that he will make them less often.

Pros approach the game differently from mere mortals. Experts concentrate on targets – specific and down to earth targets – and on the means of achieving them. 'All' they do is to decide on the kind of shot required (straight, draw, spin, etc.), identify a spot on the terrain and aim at it. Under no circumstances will they think of 'negative' areas that must be avoided, like lakes, ditches, bunkers and woods. They know that if they did, they would be punished. Ordinary golfers have a diametrically opposed attitude. They concentrate on the mechanics of the swing, on hitting the ball hard and far, and pay special attention to avoidance targets. They are extremely good at identifying trouble and make a very conscious effort to evade it. More often than not, the result is a shot straight into the hazard.

I remember one occasion very vividly. It was a knockout match between two club champions. The opponent looked harmless enough, and harmless looking opponents are always dangerous. "I've never played this course before," the lady divulged freely, "and I'd be ever so obliged, if you could point

*out to me any hazards on the course," she told our champion
with an air of sweet innocence.*

*"You mean, every hazard?" Our club champion was not
happy. It was an odd request.*

*"Yes, indeed. I stupidly forgot to buy a course planner," she
explained quite plausibly.*

*"But wouldn't it be better if you ask me, when in doubt?"
our club champion demurred.*

*"Well, if you don't wish to help me, don't bother," the lady
responded a little frostily.*

*Our champion was in a quandary. What could she do?
She was damned if she did and she was damned if she didn't.
Being a nice lady, she decided to point out the hazards. The
result would have been comical, were it not tragic. Every time
she alerted her opponent to some danger, her own ball went
straight into the hazard like a guided missile.*

- ***Conclusion:*** *consider only practical problems and what to
do about them. Never think of danger. Nothing is in play
unless you make it so.*

The impact of practice on the Inverted-U-Function is twofold: first,
it improves the performance on every level of arousal, and second,
it creates more room for manoeuvre around the point of peak
performance. The player does not fizzle out too quickly, and
becomes adept at operating constructively through troughs as well
as peaks. This is not an idle point. Both extremes are bad for the
concentration. A sudden eagle or even an unexpected birdie can be
as distracting as a triple bogey. A player needs to learn how to
handle success as well as how to handle failure. Most of all, one
needs to learn how to regain one's composure when a catastrophe
strikes like lightning.

One practises in order to perform better when it matters. But
practice and friendly games are nothing like a real competition. The

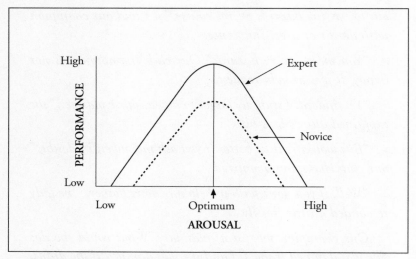

Figure 8. The impact of practice on the Inverted-U-Function

essential difference between them is, in a word, s*TRESS*. Only too often things progress smoothly without a cloud on the horizon when suddenly, for no apparent reason, golfers throw the game away. The higher the pressure to win and the higher the uncertainty attached to it, the more stressful the situation. Stress is a highly subjective matter. The more important the outcome is to the individual, the more stressful the situation becomes. The element of uncertainty is magnified by the weight the individual accords the competition.

Winning the weekly ladies competition may be fun but is hardly worth talking about. Winning the club championship or a qualifying national event is another matter. Once a well-known jeweller sponsored our ladies weekly medal. The first prize was a rather nice necklace. It was enough to transform a usually jolly medal into a tense occasion.

What to do in stressful situations is very important, but it is not something that can be easily practised. It would be plainly ridiculous to react with all the vigour, determination and, indeed, desperation of a real competition to a mere make-believe situation.

Self-knowledge is what separates the experienced golfer from the inexperienced one and gives him a very real advantage to boot.

Experience means three things:

1. That the necessary mental resources capable of coping with stress are in place.

2. That the technical aspects, especially the automatisation and routinisation of the appropriate action, have been thoroughly rehearsed.

3. That the positive factors outweigh stress.

The more experienced the player, the less vulnerable he is when the going gets tough. The pro knows that the game fluctuates. He understands that this volatility is its very nature, and is precisely what makes it so fascinating. Most important of all he accepts stoically the misfortunes inflicted upon him. But when the club golfer is persecuted by golfing demons, he deems himself victimised. He is disgusted and disillusioned, and may even indulge in a little self-pity.

Perhaps the most aggravating (and challenging) aspect of golf is its treacherous nature. Rounds which start smoothly enough can suddenly be transformed into torture chambers. The reasons are not clear, and are not always the same. Something that is highly disturbing in one game can be totally inconsequential in another.

Generally speaking, there are three types of competitions:

- Stable competitions,
- Unstable competitions, and
- Crisis-prone competitions.

They are not mutually exclusive, and one match may well lurch from one phase to another as the drama unfolds.

Stable competitions are those during which performance is powered by serene concentration, things progress smoothly and the player functions at or near optimal level. The better one plays, the easier the game becomes. Those are the days on which miracles happen as though fortune itself intercedes on your behalf. On such days your sole concern is to stand aside and enjoy that state of grace. The Zone is a golfer's paradise. Alas, such days are rare and far between.

The majority of competitions are **unstable.** A birdie can and often is followed by a double bogey, a dramatic recovery from the ditch turns sour by a missed putt. The ups and downs mirror, and are sometimes the precursors of the player's mental state, as he see-saws between bliss and disgust.

Destabilisation can be caused by a minor event: A chance remark, a wayward shot, a drop in concentration, tiredness. But once destabilisation has occurred, it reflects the effect of either **hypo-activation** or **hyper-activation.** These two mechanisms can be best understood in terms of the Inverted-U-Function.

Hypo-activation is a situation in which the player is under-aroused. He has fallen into the psyche-up zone and urgently needs the mobilisation of new resources. For instance:

- Boosting energy resources. The remedy could be something as simple as a banana, chocolate, or an energy bar.
- Adequate fluid consumption is vital.
- Invigorating breath: inhaling 'energy', exhaling waste, fatigue and stress.
- Empowering imagery and the use of energising cue words (GO! SHOOT! OMPH!).

Hyper-activation is the exact opposite. The system is overcharged and is in urgent need of calming down. Relaxation techniques are best suited to deal with wild emotions and to oversee the return to balance. For instance:

- A quick body scan, paying particular attention to tension in neck and shoulders. RELEASE.
- Tense all muscle groups. HOLD for ten second, and RELEASE.

Both hypo- and hyper-activation are negative states which require modification. Again, the experienced golfer will recognise sooner the danger signs. He will also be better equipped to mount a rescue operation. No one is immune to the vicissitudes of golf, but the alarm bells ring earlier for the experts.

Utter despair...

When destabilisation deteriorates to a point of no return, the player is in a state of crisis. Extreme physical and psychological agitation plagues his every shot. Control is lost and so is judgement. Motor performance is acutely affected. The simplest shots are strangled. A plethora of damaging and irrelevant responses choke, cram and hinder every swing. The player becomes overwrought, hostile and resentful and, sometimes, downright dangerous, especially to himself.

On All Winners Day, a five-handicapper was having a very bad day. He had hoped to win the competition which was a thirty-six-hole-haul, played on two courses. As the morning wore on, he had several opportunities to seethe in frustration.

But when he reached the sixteenth hole, he was confronted with a situation that tested his self-restraint to the extreme.

The drive ended in the face of a bunker where it hung, defying Newton's law of gravity, on the very edge propped up by a tiny twig. He stared at the ball incredulously, perhaps, secretly hoping that it would fall into the bunker, but the ball did not budge. Eventually he took a shot at it, balancing precariously outside the bunker. He overdid it and the ball flew across the green and ended in the trees beyond it. Gritting his teeth he stood under the trees and tried to find a path to the green. Another miss! The ball ricocheted wildly and bounced off several branches before it finally came back to rest at his feet.

To us, who observed him with some trepidation, it seemed that the ball was mocking him. Unprintable oaths emerged from the grove, as the hapless golfer addressed his ball once again. This time it hit a sleeper bordering the path and came back at him with full force. At this, a scream of agony issued from his lips. A look of demented venom distorted his face. With one mighty leap he reached his bag and tore out the four-iron. Facing away from the green, which was not more than six yards away, he hit a full shot back towards the tee. The ball rose powerfully, hit timber, broke off a branch, turned 180° degrees and landed smack in the middle of the green.

We hastily withdrew to a safe distance for, foaming at the mouth like a rabid animal, the man leapt on the ball, grabbed it in his hand as though to crush it, and threw it away with all his might. We had hoped that he would go away now that he was disqualified, but no, he insisted on accompanying us and playing, inflicting more and more punishment and humiliation upon himself till the bitter end.

When catastrophe strikes, the effects are likely to last for a long time. It is all very well saying 'this is only a game'. The truth is that a disastrous match gnaws at one's soul and destroys one's confidence. The main object of practice after a crisis is damage limitation. Material proof is required for the restoration of equanimity and self-belief. Most of the work must be done on the mind and the soul of the player for, after all, the technical ability is not and never was the culprit.

Two thousand five hundred years ago, the founding fathers of the Olympic Games already knew the value of fitness in everyday life. Nothing is new under the sun and there is no doubt at all that a good physical condition contributes to better performance. When Ballesteros announced that he had taken up cycling to strengthen his legs, some eyebrows were raised in astonishment: strong legs? What do they have to do with good golf? The fact is, that the fitter the player is, the better he feels and the better he plays. The more presentable he is, the better he plays. Regular visits to the gym and a keep-fit programme ought to become an integral part of practice. The PGA Tour has a mobile gym unit. Diet fanatics like Gary Player recommend suitable eating regimes. Nowadays, nothing is left to chance. There is no fun in international golf: work, work, work, early nights and, of course, a lot of money and no time to enjoy it.

SUMMARY 8: PRACTICE

1. The purpose of practice is to **learn, rehearse** and **imprint** the correct models of performance upon the mind.

2. Practice works by **transforming complex shots into simple ones,** and by **automating all shots.**

3. Practise physical and mental skills. They are both essential for optimal performance.

4. Practise regularly and systematically. Follow a plan and stick to it.

5. Review your progress and chart it.

6. **P&P:** practise and persevere.

DO-IT-YOURSELF 7: PRACTICE

ON THE RANGE:

1. Practice lasts, on average, about one hour. The more often you practise, the better will be the result. You will gain more from frequent short practice than from occasional long practice.

2. Divide practice into:
    - 40% long game,
    - 60% short game.

3. Be specific about the aspects of the long and short game to practise each time. Design your practice with care: Which woods and irons? Chipping? Putting? Bunker shots? Approach shots? Find the optimal combination.

4. Make up rules and stick to them. For instance, decide to chip into the hole and one-putt at least x times before you stop practising for the day.

5. Set a number of short distance targets on the green and chip or pitch closest to them: (a) from a bunker, and (b) from the fairway.

6. Pay particular attention to putting. It is the quickest way to improve your score and the hardest skill to maintain.

7. Practise deliberate draws and fades.

8. Over time, set harder goals.

9. Chart your progress.

ON THE COURSE:

1. Play several balls.

2. Practise nerve-wrecking shots:
    - over ponds,
    - over bunkers,

- over high trees,
- under trees,
- blind shots.

3. Record the number of times you:
   - hit the fairways,
   - reached the greens in regulation,
   - one-putted.

   Chart your progress.

4. Play eclectic competition with yourself.

5. Impose fines on three putts and on scores worse than double bogey, bogey or par, depending on your level of play. Buy your mother-in-law a present with the proceeds.

AT HOME:

1. Identify your favourite mental skills: Imagery? Self-talk? Relaxation? Concentration? Discover the blend which works best for you. Allocate 5-15 minutes daily, preferably mornings and evenings.

2. Invest in a good teaching video.

3. Putt on fast and slow surfaces at home. Aim at concrete targets.

4. Watch professional golf. Put yourself in the player's place and 'putt'. Compare his line with yours.

5: Rogues, Creeps and Bricks

On the course, a person may be cool but he is never indifferent. Golf, like the camera, has an uncanny way of X-raying the soul and putting its very essence on display. Allegedly, one learns more about another person in bed than anywhere else. The golf game, then, is only second to sex. During my years of clandestine observation on the golf course I have come to recognise the symptoms of several disorders and have identified twelve major types. Some affect the sexes equally. Others are truer of women than of men. Where gender differences exist they are denoted by the female pronoun.

1. THE HIGH PRIEST

For some, golf is not a game but a way of life. They serve at the altar of this sport with utter devotion, and generally behave with reverence more befitting a church than a field of cut grass. Golf is their religion and is treated like a sacred duty, complete with initiation rites. The history, the traditions, the folk heroes and the Byzantine rules are cultivated with fanatic fervour. The dedication it inspires in mere amateurs is proof that this is more than a game: it is a supreme test of character. The High Priest conducts himself with exemplary decorum. He epitomises the true spirit of golf by setting good standards of behaviour and by providing fair and inspiring leadership.

2. THE METRONOME

Every club has its serious players. They are easily identified by their demeanour. Before each shot they will take a practice swing. They will check their stance and address the ball meticulously. Very seldom will they rush their shots, and rarely will they allow themselves to be diverted from their established routines. On the greens, they regard the putts from all directions. They will lift a club to their face and close one eye. They will insist on total silence, and on your standing at a deferential distance from them.

There is much to admire about the metronome: the hard work, the ambition to achieve perfection and the uncompromising commitment to excellence. The metronome is fiercely competitive, and the closest that a club player ever comes to a professional player.

3. THE OBSESSED

She has a blueprint for practice which will be executed without fail, every day, in sunshine or hailstorm, no matter what. Her approach is one of surgical precision and her standards will pass any audit. She is hard on herself as she is hard on others, tension and determination entwined. On the surface she may appear to be one of the guys, but inside, a fire is burning, an all consuming furnace of ambition. Golf is her life, and lack of perspective makes her a potential candidate for a mental breakdown. She is seldom defeated, but when she is, she lacerates inwardly, broods incessantly and takes ages to recover. Victories are the tonic of her life. She assigns herself goals and pursues them relentlessly. Once one goal is achieved, a new and harder one is immediately set. In short, the lady is a fanatic, complete with some remote exalted figure for a deity. Closer to home, however, she has a friend, usually someone better at golf than herself, someone she emulates and secretly envies but, above all, someone she wishes to surpass.

4. THE PUNDIT

I personally do not know a worse type to play with. They are sweet and helpful and, oh... so obviously superior. They know exactly what is wrong with you, and they only wish to help you. I happen to believe that I am entitled to make my own mistakes without receiving unsolicited advice from others. After playing with a pundit, you are likely to develop major faults, and it will take weeks, nay months, to get over them.

Sometimes the advice is straightforward: "You're not transferring," or "your back-swing is too long." But often the criticism is veiled in hypocrisy. "That stop at the top of the swing is very effective in your case…", or "You have a very idiosyncratic putting stroke…", or "You really prefer woods, don't you…" Innocuous but poisonous. The kindest and wisest advice I was ever given by a golfer was: "Don't let anyone tamper with your swing."

5. THE GENTEEL

Some like to show that they have class. Raucous behaviour is absolutely prohibited(!) and standards of decorum will be maintained under any provocation. If the course treats them badly, if their swing goes to pieces, if the putts do not drop, they will smile sweetly and sigh. Under no circumstances will they fling their clubs or, God forbid, utter an oath. Under extreme and sustained humiliation they may just murmur: 'sugar'. Should you find yourself playing with such paragons of virtue, such models of good behaviour, do restrain yourself. Otherwise, upon returning to the club house, they will declare with a faint and delicate shudder that you are well, ahh… N.Q.O.C.D.

6. THE CHATTERBOX

Some regard golf as a tea party. Silence embarrasses them. As soon as there is a lull in the conversation they hasten to fill in the gap. They talk out of fear of appearing to be impolite. If you are a more taciturn type, you would soon find yourself an object of curious and searching glances as the other tries to decide whether you are being rude or merely monumentally dull. Depending on his conclusions, he might then talk at length without expecting any significant response from you. Finally and somewhat desperately, you would be subjected to a thorough cross-examination, the kind any prosecutor would be proud of. That would be your last chance to reveal something about yourself. Relax, there is no malice in all this, only an overwhelming need to be friendly.

The chatterbox is noisy but well-meaning. His game will fluctuate wildly from rubbish to the sublime. A round with this type is excellent training. If you can shut out the banter and the whoops, the talking while you putt and the loud sneeze while you are addressing the ball, it proves that you can achieve a high level of concentration in less than ideal circumstances, and that is good.

One day I found myself playing with a pair of twins. It was impossible for me to tell who was who, and I was never quite sure whether the right person was playing the right ball, or whose card I was marking. But that was the least of it. They were the funniest and jolliest pair of players I have ever seen. When the shot was good, they whooped: "You're a star, a champ! You're the man!" But when the shot was bad, their enthusiasm knew no bounds. "That shot was awful," I pointed out in genuine bewilderment. "What does it matter?" they retorted cheer-fully, "the rest of the field will think it was good." I realised that there was a method in their madness, aimed at demoralising the whole corps de golf with a campaign of disinformation.

7. THE WHIMP

She doggedly enters every competition, knowing full well that she will not excel, not for long anyway. On the whole, she is genuinely unpretentious and not terribly competitive. She just cannot understand what all the fuss is about. Winning or losing, what the hell, either way it was good fun. She likes to please and have a quiet life. Sweet and docile, the truth is that she is as indifferent to you as she is to the result. But some whimps are resentful, even spiteful. Pride is one of the seven deadly sins, and whimps can be guilty of spleen. To challenge directly is not their style. Instead, they fret and backbite safely out of sight. Like a little bird, the whimp darts out, pecks and departs.

8. THE PEACOCK

She is dazzling and effective and often very good looking. Her legs
are smooth and brown and her clothes – oh so smart. She is smug
and egocentric. Self-confidence propels her to success which she
judiciously regards as a tribute to herself. Like Muhammad Ali,
she psyches her opponents and encourages them to abandon the
fight: "You're going to lose. Is **that** all you can do?" Though
arrogant, she is not unlikeable and can be quite charming. But
if things go unexpectedly wrong, she is prone to an emotional
downpour.

"Women," declared the Earl of Chesterfield, "are much more
like each other than men: they have, in truth, but two passions,
vanity and love." The Earl of Chesterfield was a notorious male
chauvinist, but he is right about the peacock. Her defining characteristic is vanity, and vanity has little sustaining power.

9. THE RAGING BULL

He thinks golf is football. Like a person possessed, he curses and
kicks, and as though that were not enough, he bludgeons the
ground with his club. Calm down, do not call for the straight-
jacket, you are not in any danger. The person is not a football
hooligan, and the violence is directed against himself. He tears
himself to bits, using epithets which strike a chord with you, and
burdens you with horror stories of his immense stupidities and
pathetic incompetence.

Please, do not agree too readily. This is a call for help, a humble,
if vocal, plea for support and you should respond humanely.

10. THE SADIST

Some women golfers use the game to subjugate, dominate and
torture others. They are born sadists but behave as though sadism
was thrust upon them by The Royal and Ancient. For they practise
their cruelty under the guise of adherence to the rules.

I still remember vividly the very first time I played in an ordinary weekly ladies competition. I was an absolute beginner who had never before even been on the golf course with anyone except my husband and the professional. I was playing with a 17-handicapper, who had very little patience with novices.

The second hole was a short par 3. It consisted of a bit of rough, an artificial lake and a diabolical undulating green flanked by three bunkers. Six yards beyond the bunker at the back was out-of-bounds. It was an intimidating hole for a beginner. My first ball landed in the lake. "Play a second ball for three," the lady instructed. Her voice was pleasant. To end in the lake was a common occurrence on that hole. The second ball followed the first into the lake, and the third, and the fourth, and the fifth and sixth. "You must play another ball," she said testily, as I showed signs of faltering. She turned to the group behind and grimaced as though to say that never in her life did she witness such pathetic incompetence. I was deeply humiliated and, by that time, perilously close to tears. "Must I?" I whispered in a barely audible voice. "If you don't want to be disqualified," she retorted resolutely. To this day I do not know how I managed to hit the green with my seventh ball.

We continued to play in stony silence till we reached the tenth hole. There were rocks and shrubs in front of the tee and a large ditch running along the right side of the fairway. On the left there was a thicket. A diagonal shot was required to avoid trouble but mine flew straight into the wood. I tried to get out, but the ball kept coming back at me like in Ping-Pong. After several futile attempts, I picked up the damn thing and threw it onto the fairway, a grand distance of a few yards.

The woman tightened her lips in suppressed fury, and a hiss like a serpent's escaped her pursed mouth. She played on with grim determination. As soon as we returned to the club house she lodged a complaint with the Committee. She also demanded that I be expelled and submitted a deposition, claiming that I refused to play by the rules of the game. Luckily, the Committee took a more compassionate view of my offences and I was allowed to continue to play. It was a baptism of fire and it taught me a lesson that I have never forgotten: Beware! Sadists act out their frustrations on the golf course.

A couple of years later I found myself playing with the husband of that bitch. He was kind enough to compliment me on my game. I thanked him and remarked in passing that his wife thought that I should be expelled. He promptly put his ball in the lake...

11. THE BULLY

She must be the centre of attention. Her view of herself is exalted and quite extravagantly self-absorbed. "I" is the subject of most conversations, addressed to an attentive court. Like a benevolent despot, she is generous on occasions, and prefers to be seen as kind and just. Criticism is forbidden: she absolutely hates it, but of flattery, she can never have enough.

Her opinion is the only opinion, and those who disagree, do so at their peril. For the lady is Stalinistic, that is to say: hypersensitively suspicious and most dangerously vindictive. Avoid her, if you can.

12. THE SNEAK

The sneak will cheat. He is a master of deception, devious to the core. On the greens the ball will be replaced a little forward. In the rough it will be nudged into a better position with, what the Americans call, a foot wedge.

I once played with a nine-handicapper who was an infamous sneak. She hit a poor shot that landed among some roots not far from the green. They were large roots as thick as an arm and the apron was only two yards away. In short, like Oscar Wilde, the lady could resist anything except temptation. She took out a putter. The ball was unaddressable but I know better than to question the decisions of other golfers.

"Would you mind standing over there? I can just see you from the corner of my eye?" she requested affably enough. "Sorry," I muttered and removed myself. In that split second when I turned away, she tapped the ball forward, while still watching me. Alas, she tapped it too hard. When I looked again the ball was not in its original place, nor was it on the apron or on the green, but in the bunker.

"How did it ever get there?" she demanded crossly, looking accusingly at me. Clearly it was my fault.

"I honestly don't know," I said as puzzled as she was.

"Are you sure you didn't touch it?" she narrowed her eyes with staggering hypocrisy.

"Quite sure," said I with steely firmness. Our eyes met... It was not a good hole.

The **bandit** is a special category of sneak and has long been enshrined in golf lore. Like a miser he protects his handicap by all means known to man, including losing strategically, if needs be. Though obsessed with winning, he is choosy about what he wins. When a round goes smoothly and the score is dangerously low, the bandit will see to it that a calamity overtakes him on the last hole. He is brazen and would not hesitate to chalk up ten shots on a single hole. Like an abacus, the seasoned bandit does not make mistakes. He always knows the exact score and precisely how and when to introduce the tactical miss. If in spite of all his stratagem, the tally is still too good, he will suddenly recall with the greatest regret, that for some obscure technical reason, the card cannot be used. Hypocrisy is his second suit, and so, with alligator tears, he would unflinchingly declare: Alas! A great pity! What a shame!

The bandit is deeply suspicious and quite envious by nature. He is very vigilant and always on the lookout for cheats and swindlers. The idea that anyone can win by merit alone is to him, clearly absurd. He is always the first to accuse others of cunning, and to demand that their handicaps be forthwith cut.

The sneak is especially dangerous in matchplay and will miscount his shots and yours, and involve you in endless reconstructions. By the time you resolve the internal debate: to challenge or not to challenge, your game is ruined, whatever you decide. If you challenge, you feel like a prosecutor, and if you don't, you feel like a coward. Either way, you lose. With an unerring instinct he susses out what irks you most and uses it ruthlessly. You can never win an argument with a sneaky opponent. It diverts mental energy from playing and guarantees the success of his strategy. He is far too cunning and knows exactly what he is doing. Keep cool and get even by winning if you can. Interestingly enough, when one has a genuinely horrid day, a sneaky remark can focus one's mind wonderfully. A rush of adrenaline and, suddenly, everything finds its proper place.

———————

No, I have not forgotten the great majority of club players, who are there to have a good time, to engage in a healthy activity and to meet people. I have not forgotten their decency and amiability and what good sports they are, especially when the chips are down. They perform the initiation rites for the new players and have the patience, the compassion and the understanding to extend a helping hand, to offer advice and simply be great pals. Hip, Hip Hurray to the backbone of any club worth its salt.

6: Women Playing With Men

O! What men dare do!

What men may do!

What men daily do,

Not knowing what they do!

(Shakespeare, *Much Ado About Nothing*)

MEN, GOLF AND MONEY

Playing with or against women brings out the best and the worst in men.

The Macho thinks a woman's place is in bed, or else, in the kitchen and nursery, not on the golf course. Kipling strikes a deep chord with the macho: "A woman is only a woman, But a good cigar is smoke." He does not enjoy playing with women and lets you know it as soon as you arrive on the first tee. On the course, he is brusque and aggressively silent, only talking when he has to. He will do his utmost to bully you into submission, and will not shy away from snide remarks. Losing is bad enough, but losing to a mere woman is purgatory. As a partner, he expects to lead and be obeyed. If you perform well, he will treat you with grudging respect; if you don't, better get out of his way.

The Nervous Wreck is a useless partner and a pathetic opponent. He casts himself in the role of the mouse helping the lioness and lets you do most of the work. The wreck dreads being outshone and, yet, acts as if dependent. When he finds himself in a corner, he will cheat with little hesitation. If he wins, he'll buy you a drink. If he loses, he'll be grumpy. Either way, it's best to get rid of him quickly.

The Gallant is confident and charming, and as a partner, a godsend. He is strong and loyal and will support you through thick and thin. His demeanour will not alter even if you blunder and put everything at risk. To him, golf is a marvellous game, not a torture chamber. To challenge him is dangerous. He will do his very best to win, but if he fails, he will compliment you sincerely and warn that tomorrow is another day.

In England, playing with women on equal footing is regarded as dangerously revolutionary. It is one thing to entrust the Country, its heritage, or the peace process in Northern Ireland to the care of women, and quite another to treat them as equals on the golf course. "Oh dear, who's ever heard of such a thing… as long as we keep the men happy, everything will be fine. We must not do anything to upset them," the Ladies Captain solemnly instructed the members of her Committee. Even today, there are clubs – like Augusta – which do not admit women. There are courses on which women are not allowed unless escorted by a male member, and there are clubs – like Sunningdale – where women are officially designated as second class members, without voting rights. Some clubs have separate entrances, separate lounges, separate bars, and generally practise total segregation of club facilities, with the notable exception of the restaurant. Club competitions are men's competitions. Women have their own section, ruled very correctly indeed by an all female committee. Over the years, in spite of considerable dragging of feet, women have made significant progress, of which the right to reserve the first tee for a limited period on Ladies Day takes pride of place. Only the Green keeper and his staff are yet to recognise the weekly ladies competitions as official, instead of an excellent day for major maintenance work on the course.

I do not say all this out of indignation – I know my place – but to explain, why a man playing with a woman cannot fail to regard her as inferior to himself. Strong or weak, when it comes to women and golf, men join Nietzsche in the plea: "May we fall into their arms without falling into their hands."

The plain truth is that there is no equality on the golf course. "Laura Davies hits the ball as far as a man." No man would be acclaimed for hitting the ball as far as Laura Davies. Jan Stephenson is said to "look like a woman but to play like a man." Even the legendary Nancy Lopez does not enjoy the same status as one of the great male stars, not even those who were put out to pasture.

In 1996, nearly 700 hours of the PGA Tour, Senior Tour and Nike Tour were broadcasted on American television. They were seen in more than 100 million homes. The main events were transmitted to nearly 100 countries. In 1997, a Ryder Cup year, the figures soared to an average of three hours of golf every day somewhere on television. The media coverage of ladies events is only a fraction of men's events. The ratio is allegedly one-to-twenty. The result is that professional women golfers are not terribly well known to the public at large.

When it comes to money and sponsorship, the ladies are so far behind the men as to be virtually out of sight. In the USA every man in the top thirty money-winners is earning, at least, $1,000,000 a year from sponsorship alone. Some earn significantly more. The exact amounts companies spend on sponsorship deals are well-guarded secrets. According to figures published in the Guinness Book of Golf, Greg Norman received $8 million, Arnold Palmer at the age of 62(!) got $9 million, Jack Nicklaus – also not a youngster – $7 million, Nick Faldo, at least, $9 million, and Tiger Woods, upon becoming a professional and before winning any major competition – a mind-boggling $43 million. The next big star is surely the incredibly gifted Justin Rose. Unknown but promising young professionals have no trouble raising as much as $60,000 a year from various sponsors.

Prize money in the European tour was approximately £30 million in 1995. In America, the three main tours – The PGA, the Nike and the Senior – are worth more than $120 million. In 1994, the Nike Tour was created to allow those who failed to qualify for the PGA Tour a chance to play. Prize money in the Nike's first year was $5.7 million, and players of total obscurity could win a quarter of a million dollars and more. During the same year, 'semi retired' golfers competed for more than $5 million on the Senior Tour. Hale Irwin, 'the best senior player in the world' won more than two

million dollars in 1998. Back in 1995, in the US PGA Tour
Championship, every player was guaranteed a minimum of
$48,000, and the first prize was a staggering $540,000. A year
later, the winner took home $630,000, and in 1997 – $720,000.
Every event on the US PGA Tour has a purse of at least $1 million.
Of the approximately $170 million won worldwide, 80% goes to
just three hundred golfers.

Golf is serious money. During the twenty-one years of Deane
Beman's stewardship as the Tour Commissioner, the revenues of the
US PGA grew dramatically from $730,000 to $200 million. In
1996, they exceeded $300 million. In the process, players became
multi-millionaires. In 1997, the top all-time money winner on the
US Tour was Greg Norman with $11.9 million. He was followed
closely by Tom Kite with $10.3 million and Fred Couples with
$8.9 million. Back in the lean year of 1991 Greg Norman's win-
nings were a mere $320,000 – a new definition of the poverty line.
All-time money winners on the European Tour are not far behind.
Bernard Langer comes first with £6.0 million, closely followed by
Colin Montogomerie with £5.99 million.

Beside prize money and sponsorship there is virtually an
unlimited supply of goods and equipment. And in addition to all
this, there is also appearance money. The usual charge paid for a
'walk' with a top international is, allegedly, $60,000. The situation
can be quite grotesque. *The Ultimate Encyclopedia of Golf* quotes a
case of a golfer who received $200,000 for appearing, while the first
prize was only $140,000. In the event, that player did not even
make the cut.

By comparison the Ladies' tour in Europe is a muted affair. As
late as 1980 only three major sponsors invested in professional
women golfers. They were Carlsberg, Hitachi and Volvo. The
total prize money for twenty-one events was a paltry £110,000.
There were signs, however, that things were changing. In 1995,
American Express safeguarded the Women's Professional Golfers
European Tour with a three-year deal, worth $3 million, which
has now ended. In 1997 McDonald chipped in with a purse of

£300,000 for the WPGA Championship of Europe at Gleneagles. During the same year, Weetabix sponsored the Ladies' British Open Championship to the tune of £525,000 pounds. Suddenly, players from all over the world, including the US, Japan and Australia flocked to Sunningdale in Surrey to take part in the tournament. But 1997 ended on a stormy note. The European Tour lost its chief executive officer, his deputy and its sponsor, American Express.

The Ladies Professional Golfers Tour in America is much more prosperous. In 1994, it had a total purse of just over $24 million, but things were set to improve. For instance, in 1995 there were eighteen events, in 1996 – twenty-two, and in 1997 – thirty seven. In stark contrast to European events, the first prize on the US LPGA Tour averages around $90,000 dollars. Top ladies are not paupers. Patty Sheehan and Pat Bradley each won about $5 million by the end of 1995 and are still going strong. In 1996, Karrie Webb was the first woman golfer to earn more than one million dollars in one year, surpassing even Laura Davies and Annika Sorenstam, who ranks number one in the world. In 1997, Annika rose to the challenge and won $1.2 million dollars. Winning the United States Ladies' Open Championship in 1997, Alison Nicholas became $232,000 richer, a substantial amount by any standard. Karrie Webb got only £82,000 for winning the Ladies' British Open Championship in the same year. In a startling contrast, the total purse for the German Ladies' Open Championship was a trifling £100,000 and the top prize, a ridiculous £15,000. Only five of the fourteen events on the European Tour offered a winning purse greater than £20,000.

Not only do men regard women as inferior, women do too. This attitude has been cultivated over centuries of socialisation. In psychology, socialisation does not refer to the art of making friends and influencing people, but to learning and internalising a set of rules about one's roles in life. Alas, the superiority of men over women is a law of nature, and possibly even more widespread than the incest taboo in all known cultures.

The great social changes of the second half of the 20th century have left their imprint on every walk of life, but have swept ever so lightly over the green fairways and the great institution of the golf club. Perhaps with good reason. Men **are** better golfers. Their game is more dramatic and, therefore, more exciting. Compare a woman and a man of the same handicap, and you will find that there is little resemblance in their game. The man is much longer and can extricate himself from all manner of trouble much better than any woman. Women are less wild but even that does not guarantee that they will score better.

MEN AS PARTNERS

In mixed pairs it is always incumbent upon the woman to be delicate, tactful and mindful of the man's ego. When he is good — praise him, but when he is bad, let him know that in your view, at least, he can do no wrong. When you play well and he plays poorly — laud his little achievements. Never ever imply criticism in word, demeanour, tone or look. And never resort to thunderous silences. Even when playing with one's own husband, when some licence is inevitable, it is best to stick to praise. Seek to calm, not to blame.

Never give unsolicited advice and never demand anything of your partner, not even in a jest. To tell him, "We need a par," when he has just shanked into the ditch, is not the way to go about it. Even when the demand is perfectly reasonable, it must not be voiced. Remember, your partner is already doing his best.

When a man plays with a woman, he risks much more than she does. Unless she is a champ, she is not supposed to play exceptionally well, and if per chance she does, it is wonderful and lucky. On the other hand, when a man plays poorly, it is a reflection upon his manhood, something, I am sure you would agree, much deeper and more wounding than a 'bad day'. I know men who were so upset over losing a match that they required professional help.

In 1993 Burgner and Hewstone conducted a fascinating research on the perceptions that men and women have about themselves.

They found that:

- Women regularly underestimate their ability, while men consistently overestimate it.

- When men succeed, they claim that they have done so because they are competent. When they fail, it is not their fault.

- Women attribute their success to luck, and when they fail they take the blame.

Most amazingly, at the tender age of five, boys and girls already mirror adult perceptions about gender differences. From an early age of cognition women learn to regard themselves as having less power than men, and their experience of life tends to reinforce this early learning. And that is not all. Nideffer discovered that men are more intellectually expressive whatever that may mean, and, in line with popular wisdom, more reticent in showing affection.

In defeat women are more gracious but men are more honest. "Good luck in the next round," a woman will intone politely even if in her heart she wishes you dead. Resentment and pique are kept under firm control. Men, on the other hand, can become indignant, childish and, sometimes, downright petty. The only time men accept defeat with an aura of nonchalance, is during the annual contest against the ladies, where a loss can be attributed to chivalry as opposed to incompetence.

Mixed pair competitions resemble marriage. When things go well, it is a honeymoon. When they go sour, it is much like divorce. And the periods between the two are just like marriage after the initial rapture has cooled off. Discussing partner's performance with others is almost as crass as commenting on someone's performance in bed. It is simply taboo.

Faithfulness during the match is vital. Nothing is more exasperating than your own partner chatting up the 'other woman', and praising her more warmly or more sincerely than he does you. Equally, if you seem to have undue interest in the 'other man', the inherent rivalry between men over established, even if temporary, territorial rights will soon manifest itself with some unexpected results.

Lyndon Johnson was reputed to be a very physical man. To emphasise his points he had a habit of pawing and touching his interlocutors. There are men who behave like Lyndon Johnson on the golf course. When my partner and I were playing in the Semi-Final of the mixed pairs, one such man was our opponent. He was well-built and exuberant. Had I stopped to think about it, I might have found him attractive. Not that this kind of thoughts usually occupy my mind during a match. It ought to be explained at the outset that in all the time that we had been playing together, my part-ner had never shown the least interest in me as a woman. But on this occasion, things were different. No sooner did our opponent arrive than I found myself afloat in mid air as though I were an elfin ballerina. When he finally set me down on terra firma he did it gently. His lips caressed my cheek with something more like a kiss than a peck. His part-ner looked studiously away. Now, my partner, who was a reticent sort of chap, marched up to the lady and kissed her. I looked studiously away, but it did not escape my attention that she literally purred before returning the kiss with some enthusiasm, and I found that disturbing.

Once on the course, the two men were soon trying to outdo each other, not in golfing prowess but in eliciting shrieks of delight and simulated horror from their female opponents. The match became a contest figuratively speaking of horns and fangs, something resembling more David Attenborough's Trials of Life than The Age of Innocence.

Things further deteriorated when the ladies themselves entered the spirit of the game and began to play one man against the other. At one point, my partner and the other woman disappeared in the bushes, manifestly looking for her ball, and took an inordinately long time to come out.

At the halfway hut, the other lady went in to powder her nose. Our gallant opponent wasted no time. He put his arm around my shoulders rather possessively, I thought, and whispered loudly enough for my partner to hear: "Will you be my partner next year?" Before I could think of an appropriate answer in the circumstances, my man retorted sharply: "No, she won't, she has a partner already!" I looked up and saw that he was very angry. But then, what gave him the right to be indignant after the way that he had been carrying on? Mercifully, the lady returned and saved us from further complications. The game resumed.

The result of the match does not matter. One pair went forward, and predictably lost in the final. Soon the two partnerships were dissolved and my partner and the other lady got together ... Of course, such goings-on are rare. Matches are usually conducted in an atmosphere of dull respectability and purposeful determination.

When playing in partnership, it is wise not to expect too much, but to be ready to do one's very best, no matter what happens. That is the spirit in which the best matches are played. Of course, on the day anything can happen and everyone, including you and me, is fallible. Often, the harder one tries, the worse one plays, and the more one struggles to extricate oneself from a horrible situation, the more deleterious the situation becomes. Dennis Healey once said, that if you find yourself in a hole, stop digging. This advice is as sound on the golf course as it is in politics.

Critical comment or shows of displeasure are *interdit!* First, the 'offenders' already suffer enough because of their own mistakes and the feeling that they are letting their partner down. And second, it is simply the most ineffective way of galvanising them into action, or putting them back on track. A word of comfort, a praise, and above all, a genuine demonstration that the mistake does not matter a hoot are far better ways to save the match. These are the building blocks upon which a good partnership thrives. Never patronise your partner when he is playing poorly. Support him, and expect him to do the same when you have a bad day.

Patronising and supporting are two very different things: the former smacks of superiority and condescension, the latter promises loyalty and friendship even if the match is lost. In short, "don't do unto others what you don't want them to do unto you." I am still grateful to the man who, when I played abominably, took me to one side and said: "remember that I want you to be my partner next year."

MEN AS OPPONENTS

A head to head contest between a man and a woman rarely occurs in England, though mixed competitions abound. In the rest of the world, women and men are equal on the golf course, if nowhere else. The first thing to understand is that it is easier for a woman to lose to a man, than vice versa. Paradoxically, it means that she enters the match at a disadvantage. There is no sense of enemy as D.H. Lawrence said – only of a disaster. It is, somehow, improper and unladylike to go all out to challenge a man and crush him; and because defeat does not mean loss of face, she does not try as hard to win. For a man to lose to a woman, especially if she is not a first class player, is like castration. At the very least, it is a public humiliation and proof that he is not the man he used to be. In mixed pairs, the margins are blurred and individual contribution to the final result is less clear. But in singles, when you lose, you lose, and there is no one else to blame but yourself.

A pair of lovers found themselves playing against each other. The woman was the better player, but after eight holes, she was already four down. He was playing well, but had he played badly, he would still have won. She just could not bring herself to beat him. Too much was at stake: his pride, his manhood, his love. It was not worth risking so much for so little. So she did not. There was no conscious decision to let him win, no rigging of the results, but psychological paralysis ruled out victory. It is far easier to play against people to whom one is not related, and easier still to play against complete strangers.

- **Conclusion:** *The less personal involvement one has with the opponent the better it is for one's game.*

A man losing to a woman would be a subject of gentle mockery. There will be oblique insinuations that he was not man enough, or else his mind was on other things. The malicious would imply that ladies, even the most virtuous ones, are possessed of little devious ploys to get their way by other means than a good swing.

I once found myself playing against a very tough man, who was less than scrupulously honest. When a lost ball miraculously reappeared on the edge of the fairway, I said nothing at all, though it had not been there when we looked for it just a few moments beforehand. Still, I did not feel that I could question his word without appearing petty, over-suspicious and downright insulting. I decided to let the matter go. It was not pure cowardice on my part. I calculated that he might think that I did not know that he cheated. But he knew, and so did his caddy... We played on.

Three holes later he bent down to place the ball on the tee when, suddenly, his trousers split open. They did not tear a little bit, but were ripped apart from belt to groin as though by an invisible hand. A posterior clad in white cotton protruded from the gap. "Aha," I said to myself, "divine intervention!" He clutched at his behind, trying to hold the flaps together but with little success. "Do you have a safety pin?" he asked in a desperate sort of way. I searched in my bag but could not find one. "It might be dangerous to stick it in there," I felt obliged to point out, trying to be helpful. In the end, he had to go all the way back to the club house in search of another pair of trousers. I waited patiently for his return. Though I was two down, I was confident that the match was as good as won.

Of course we never heard the end of it. The members took the mickey out of us, and wanted to know precisely what caused the trousers to split so dramatically. What could possibly be the reason for such rupture in a pair of breeches? Ha, ha, ha!

An interesting study on rule violation found that people under stress cheat more. Since a man playing against a woman is under greater pressure to win, he will be tempted to resort to underhanded methods when the match goes against him. How should a woman deal with such a situation? With equanimity, for best effect. If she has the nerve, she may challenge the man, if not there is always the hope that an invisible hand will tear his trousers apart. Miracles do happen!

7: Matchplay

THE JEWEL IN THE CROWN

Matchplay is the jewel in the crown of golf. It extracts the best and the worst from the soul of its practitioners because it is the sternest test of character. Matchplay is different from other types of competition in three crucial respects.

1. Golf is an individualistic game, a strictly private matter between oneself and the course. But in matchplay one is not battling only against the elements. There enters an opponent to reckon with, someone who is both adversarial and threatening. It is one thing to struggle against oneself and lose, and quite another matter to lose to a third party. From a private affair, it becomes a public one with all the repercussions that this simple shift in emphasis entails. The situation is rather like playing chess against the computer as opposed to playing against a 'live' opponent.

2. Matchplay is deceptively forgiving. Mistakes count but not as much as in stroke play. One may massacre a few holes and still go on to win the match. Losing to a birdie is the same as taking a quadruple bogey. Hope springs eternal, and as long as there are enough holes to play, anything, but absolutely anything can happen.

3. To win at matchplay, you do not need to play well. You only need to play better than the opponent. If you are strong enough to raise your game when the chips are down, if you never admit defeat, you will win more often than you lose. Matchplay is about character, not about the ability to play.

Once out on the golf course nothing exists except the opponent and you. Like two cocks pitted against each other, it is a struggle between two wills. *"Victoire, c'est la volonté,"* said Marshal Foch, "My centre is giving way, my right is in retreat; situation excellent. I shall attack." Barring exceptional circumstances, technical ability

alone will not win a match. In any event, the difference in compet-
ence is either small or taken care of by the handicapping system. But
the handicap does not reflect the will to win and the strength of
character which are the cardinal factors in matchplay. Nor does it
reflect the depth of one's reserves and the ability to call upon new
resources when all seems lost. No one is invincible, and even the
most formidable opponent may have an off day.

In this head to head confrontation every act is calculated to
achieve ultimate victory, beginning with the foreplay. Have you
noticed how two opponents size each other up surreptitiously? How
they delve into each other's records and research their form and
their reputation? Have you noticed how each strives to exude that
aura of nonchalance and quiet confidence, while watching intently
the competitor for telltale signs of nerves? And while watching,
little hints are dropped, a kaleidoscope of conflicting messages. I am
not talking about cheating or even gamesmanship, which is a mild
form thereof, but about the proper utilisation of one's resources
in preparation for battle. Like a good general, this one-person
squadron, is using planning, bluff, camouflage, inscrutability and
intelligence to maximise the chances of victory.

GAMESMANSHIP

More gamesmanship is employed in matchplay than in any other
form of golf, precisely because psychology is half the match. Gamesmanship is defined by the Webster Dictionary as "the art of winning
games by doubtful expedients without actually violating the rules".
Six are the weapons employed and both sexes are accomplished
practitioners of this nefarious art.

Nagging: The trickster will vex you with complaints, the pettier the
better. He will accuse you of making a noise when you have not, or
complain that you arrived late. Wherever you are on the golf course
is wrong, and whenever you move, you are told off. There will be
countless grumbles about the slowness of the people ahead, about

the rudeness of the people behind, the weather, the state of the greens and, of course, about your handicap.

Sabotage: The trickster will remark in passing on your clothes, or your hair, or your swing, and make you feel terribly self-conscious. He will spontaneously recall a best forgotten, ancient incident, one at which you did not shine. Affably enough, he will comment in passing that you have − or have not − mastered *that* bunker shot. As a matter of principle he will be reluctant to give even short putts, and most disconcertingly of all, he will, for no good reason at all, suddenly question your veracity.

Praise: The trickster will extol your virtue and smother you with praise till you are completely demoralised. He will profess to stand no chance and to be resigned to this gloomy prospect. Somehow, he will obliquely suggest, that your handicap is surprisingly high and will, no doubt, soon come tumbling down. His admiration is a poison chalice, designed to make you feel guilty and throw you off your guard. Do not succumb.

Advice: When you find yourself in trouble, the trickster will be most solicitous. He will rush to the spot as though carried on the

Gamesmanship ...

wings of hope. And before you have time to consider the problem and come to any decision, he will offer advice and voice an opinion about the tough shot you need to contemplate. He will take it upon himself to tell you exactly what to do – or not to do – and subtly suggest that you ignore his advice at your peril. Just remember, he implies, this is a favour and you ought to be grateful. When you attempt something 'incredible', he will seek refuge behind a thick tree. "Are you done yet?" he will crow, just as you address the ball, and even without seeing that look on his face, you know that he thinks you can't do it.

Sympathy: Before any shot is played, you will learn that he is ill, that he is suffering from a hangover and has a splitting headache, or that he has just returned from a trip and is terribly jet-lagged. To make matters worse, there is trouble with the wife and the boss. If your opponent happens to be female, you will learn that the central-heating has collapsed and the plumber did not turn up. The dog was hit by a car. Her son is ill, the poor boy is feverish and alone at home. It was really terribly inconvenient to play at such a time. You will learn of all her afflictions, and feel rotten that you can't empathise. The best ploy ever played on me was in a final of the ladies single matchplay. "Let me win," my opponent said disarm-ingly as we stood waiting for our turn on the first tee. "I'm old and this is my last chance. You're young and you will have plenty of opportunities in the future." I am telling you the truth. This is not a joke. It actually happened to me! And the result was predictable. I could not hit even one good shot and lost more balls than in a whole year. She was an old fox.

Never ever look dejected or muffed, and never ever complain about any real malaise. It is all grist to the trickster's mill. His sympathy is phoney; his condolences are at best superficial and smug. Like Anna in *The King and I,* whistle a happy tune when you are down.

Browbeating: The trickster will boast about past achievements and hint at present greatness. He or she is terribly busy! A captain of this or that, a member of every squadron. Oh dear, so many demands and such precious little time to do justice to them all. He will look mildly censorious, bemused and, above all, in control. His condescending look suggests that you'd do better to give up right then and there. He is far too good to be seriously challenged by the likes of you. Superiority and proven excellence give him the right to victory. Your sole duty, he tacitly implies, is to oblige his Royal Highness with a bow.

Everything in matchplay is potentially upsetting. The difference between the trickster and the honest player is that he uses gamesmanship as a deliberate technique. Every arrow is a polished diamond, every action is calculated to draw blood. There is no defence against gamesmanship. The bravest knights have fallen victim to it. The very attempt to steel oneself against it, aggravates the symptoms. To ignore it, one must be superhuman or entirely obtuse, possibly both. Gamesmanship cannot touch you only when your consciousness is raised to the stratosphere of concentration, and that does not happen every day.

TACTICS

"Know Thyself," is the motto of the oracle of Delphi. Know your game, know your strengths and, above all, know your weaknesses. There is a famous story about an ordinary club player who challenged the legendary Arnold Palmer to a match. He made only one stipulation: that the game be played at midnight. The man was blind.

Some things can drive one to distraction. For instance, fidgeting on the tee while you are addressing the ball, or 'practising out of eyesight', excruciatingly slow play, and, indeed, incessant chatting, one of Lee Trevino's lethal weapons.

- *Should any such **potentially** disturbing problems be raised in advance?*

The trouble with attempting to pre-empt potential problems is that they may not arise. Meanwhile, one's Achilles' Heel has been exposed to the secret delight of the opponent. On the other hand, waiting till something happens and then agonising whether to mention the problem is sapping. Moreover, an unscrupulous opponent may take sadistic pleasure in torturing you and forcing you to repeat your complaint time and time again, knowing only too well how destabilising this is. If the matter is settled before any incident takes place, it becomes – one hopes – a binding agreement, and if it is violated, the pressure is on the offending party.

> *Once, just when I was about to drive, my opponent sneezed loudly. The ball went straight into the woods. "I'm most awfully sorry," she piped, but carefully refrained from suggesting that I take another shot. With some difficulty I composed myself. Accidents like this do happen. It was just bad luck. On the next tee all was quiet, but on the following one, she blew her nose. "I hope it didn't bother you," she cooed sweetly. I now began to fear interference even if none was coming.*
>
> *The shots became rushed. I summoned all my courage and said: "I know you're not doing it deliberately, but do you mind awfully keeping quiet when I am addressing the ball?" "Sure, no problem," she said with a fiendish smile, and most obligingly did not. Instead, she took to standing on the tee, just within eye range, tapping her foot ever so lightly as though impatient to get on with the job. She did not make any noise but the effect was as loud as any sneeze. I lost the match.*

On balance, I think, it is best to take one's chances and adopt a 'wait and see' approach. But, if things occur which are absolutely crucial to your well-being on the course, do not procrastinate and raise them at once. Better still, desensitise yourself, if you can, against the most frequent stressors.

- *What attitude should one adopt when the rules are not absolutely clear?*

This is a tricky question. Is this a rabbit burrow, or merely a hole in the ground? Is this ordinary shit, or a burrowing animal's shit? Is it rough, or the very edge of the fairway? Is it a giveable putt, or not? One plays out of turn, do you demand a replay? In my opinion, it is always better to be lenient and err on the side of generosity. This is not weakness or stupidity. Nor, indeed, is it chivalry. Bloody-mindedness creates tension which affects both parties. It is the surest way to transform a rival into a demon. Forbearance rarely costs a match and, with a bit of luck, will make the opponent less inclined to go for your throat.

- *What is the ideal frame of mind?*

The importance of mental and physical preparation cannot be overstated. Practice, performance routines, relaxation techniques are the building blocks of good performance. Above all, the level of arousal must be kept in check. Golf is not sex and too much arousal is bad for the game. What is required is not the zest of war and the cry of battle, but control. Matchplay is not won or lost on the first hole. Things may happen which will test you to the extreme. You may need to dredge your soul for strength and inspiration. Do not squander your reserves on cocky displays, on bravado and bad temper – you are not Muhammad Ali or McEnroe, and golf is not boxing or tennis. Nervous foreboding is as distracting as titillated anticipation. They are both forms of self-indulgence and are best avoided. Keep cool baby and, as Peter Alliss advises, win slowly.

- *Is it better to be up or down?*

Naturally, one would love to have an easy match. Alas, the opponent may not oblige. There is more to winning a match than playing the better golf. In some ways, it is preferable to be down than up after the first few holes. It lulls the opposition into false confidence and keeps the 'loser' on his toes. There is a perilous tendency to relax when things are going well, a luxury which does not exist when one is behind. I will not go as far as to say that it is better to be down as a matter of tactics only because there is no assurance that one will be able to regain the momentum. The one thing you must not do, even when the situation seems desperate, is give up. Never think of defeat! Continue to fight and be committed to it. Remember: as long as there are enough holes left, there is a chance and anything might happen.

The result of any particular match can never be taken for granted. Complacency is the worst possible mistake in matchplay. The weaker the opponent, the more dangerous he is because he has nothing to lose and everything to gain. The stronger you are the more humiliating a defeat will be, and so the pressure to win is on you. Imagine playing against Tiger Woods. If you win, it would be an astonishing victory, a memory to cherish and relate to your children and grandchildren. If you lose, however, it would be perfectly normal and as it should be. There is no glory for Tiger in beating the likes of you and me.

Once, minutes before a fairly important county match was due to start, our Captain said something to me which still today, years later, rankles. What she said does not matter, but it was enough to shatter that delicate balance, which is so essential for good golf. I stood on the first tee, took careful aim and swung. The ball trickled a few yards on the ground as though kicked by a clumsy child. It was the beginning of a nightmare. I tried very hard to swing properly. I kept my head down, took a few deep breaths, did my best to slow down. But nothing helped. The harder I tried the worse it got. After a few holes of my hacking away, my opponent concluded not surprisingly that I was a pushover. I saw her watching me with puzzled amazement. Was it possible that some mistake was made and she was playing against a complete beginner?

"Have you been playing long?" she asked unable to contain her curiosity any longer. She could not understand how I was selected for the team.

"No, I'm just having a very bad day," I replied lamely.

Her eyebrows shot to her hair line as though to say that 'a bad day' was the understatement of the year.

I was taking so many shots and losing so many balls that we had to allow all the matches behind us to pass, and we were now the last on the course. After nine holes I was six down, only saved from total ruin by some mistakes she made. As we passed the club house, a crony of hers came to investigate the state of the match. She was pulled to one side and was given the splendid news. "Six up! Well done!" I overheard the lady exclaim in an astonished whisper. We continued to play. I managed to halve the next two holes and after the eleventh I was still six down. All she needed to do was to halve a couple of holes to win the match, and that did not seem unduly ambitious the way things were going.

At that point a yawning gap opened between us and the match ahead, and my opponent, conscious of her team mates waiting for the result, sent an emissary to the club house with the message: "Go tell them that I have won." I was astounded. In all probability she was right, but to announce a victory before it was won? To this day, I do not know exactly what switched me back into gear, but I started to play better, much better. She lost the twelfth, the thirteenth, the fourteenth, the fifteenth and the sixteenth. I did not spare a second to think about her mental state, but standing on the seventeenth tee, I knew that I must win this hole. No sooner did the thought cross my mind and all the faults of the first nine holes returned with a vengeance. I hooked my drive into the woods and was only able to halve the hole but, somehow, I managed to win the eighteenth.

It was late and they were waiting for us impatiently to come in. The possibility that the game was not over did not even enter their heads. The two teams crowded at the windows, watching us with shocked stupefaction as we turned away from the club house and went back to the first tee. The tension was palpable. Everyone came running out to watch us. We carried on in grim silence and we halved every hole till number five, a par three. There, learning something from my mistakes in the morning, I went in with the 5-wood and put the ball on the green near the hole. It was too much for my opponent, and when I birdied the hole, the match was at last over.

To me that match encapsulated everything that matchplay is. My opponent did not lose simply because I suddenly switched gears and started to play better. That was the minor reason. She lost primarily because the most treacherous thought in the game, the one thought that must be nipped in the bud, the thought that she was winning, entered her mind. A game is never won before it is over. Indeed, the quickest route to defeat is the perfidious certainty of victory. When one is six up, it is almost inhuman not to indulge in the thought of triumph, but it must be squashed, eradicated, strangled before it poisons the mind.

It has been reported that when John Daly watched Costantino Rocca stunningly fluff his approach shot to the eighteenth green in the 1995 British Open, leaving him with a monstrous 60-foot putt to force a play-off, he stood up and called for his windproof jacket. John Daly must have been the only person in the world who knew absolutely that Rocca would do it. This is the hallmark of the expert. The experienced player will know from bitter experience how ephemeral are early gains and how dangerous it is to count your chickens before they are hatched. It has a most deleterious effect on the arousal level. The intoxication of anticipated victory psyches the player out of range, and in no time at all, performance plummets and concentration evaporates. A commanding lead is nibbled at and shrinks and, suddenly, a seemingly invincible position becomes very vulnerable indeed. Soon, the 'victor' is under cruel pressure to hang on and fight for something he believed was his and suddenly is no more. The switch from the psychological state of 'winner' to 'loser' is devastating, and all the more brutal for being so abrupt. **"From the sublime to the ridiculous, there is only one step,"** proclaimed Napoleon after the debacle in Moscow. To be cheated out of a 'sure' victory is worse than a straight loss.

SUMMARY 8: MATCHPLAY

1. Matchplay is played against the course, yourself and an opponent. It is the toughest test of character and a cruel contest of wills.

2. Complacency even in a seemingly invincible position is taboo. A Match is never lost – or won – till it is over.

3. Be kind but firm. It is better to be over generous than a stickler for the rules.

4. Gamesmanship is the art of winning games by doubtful expedients without actually violating the rules. The expedients are:

   • nagging,
   • sabotage,
   • praise,
   • advice,
   • sympathy,
   • browbeating.

5. There is no foolproof protection against gamesmanship, but concentration and self-talk might help.

8:   Winners And Losers

Nobody is bigger than the game of golf itself.
(Lynne Truss, *The Times*).

No one enters a competition with the intention of losing. Both winners and losers do their best to win. And, yet, some do well with monotonous regularity with only occasional lapses, while others, quite as regularly, do poorly. The concept of the 'born winner' implies that something beyond the player's technical ability is responsible for his winning. That something is an unshakeable belief in oneself, a fearless pursuit of victory, a ruthless streak and a killer's instinct. Earl Woods, Tiger Woods' father, described his son's qualities in chilling bluntness: "He's totally ruthless. No quarter asked. None given … He'll cut your throat in a heartbeat and then watch you bleed to death."

Winners score high on **self-efficacy** (the gauge which measures one's confidence in one's ability to cope in specific situations). Albert Bandura conducted extensive studies about winners, which confirmed the importance of self-efficacy. He discovered that winners are:

- More committed,
- Choose tougher goals,
- Never give-up, and
- Blame failure on lack of sufficient effort.

Winners actually prefer challenging matches to easy ones, and they also do better in them. They are driven by an insatiable hunger to scale new heights.

In contrast, losers score low on self-efficacy. They are:

- More anxious,
- Choose easier goals,
- 'Tank', that is give-in mentally and stop trying, and
- Blame failure on lack of ability.

Performance in any one competition is, by definition, unique. But the standard of achievement over time depends to a surprising extent on the player's track record. There will always be the surprise winner, the rookie who wins out of the blue, the one-off magician who dazzles for a moment and fizzles out like a fading firework. But enduring success is something else. It rests not on a whim and a chance but on solid foundation, which is a mixture of talent, hard work, character and destiny. Sustained success comes to those who were born to win. The more they win the more likely they are to continue to win, till the bell tolls for them too. Jack Nicklaus had 18 major wins, double the second best record held by Gary Player.

What separates the winner from the loser? Inner grit and the refusal to accept defeat are both important, but they are not enough. Losers are not synonymous with bad players! What stopped Greg Norman, a man not known for faintheartedness, from winning the 1996 Masters in spite of a commanding lead? Above all, his track record as the man who was on the verge of winning many times but did not. A big fish he may be, but Moby Dick he is not. Something in the situation put his memory tape on 'play', and it played with cruel precision all those times, when defeat was snatched from the jaws of victory: Bob Tway's amazing winning of the PGA 1986, when Norman had a 5-shot lead with nine holes to play, David Frost's famous bunker shot in New Orleans, Larry Mize's 100-yard pitch that went straight into the hole in the enthralling sudden death in Augusta. Greg Norman remembered that he was the best golfer in the world who won only two majors (the 1986 and 1993 British Opens). He remembered, most of all, how Faldo defeated him in 1990 at St. Andrews. There he was, forty-one years of age, the great white shark, on his sixteenth attempt to win the Masters. And from that subconscious stream followed the most effective sequence of shots which paved the way to another defeat, perhaps, the most devastating of his career. It was not what Nick did to Greg but what Greg did to himself.

Winners can be charming, even magnanimous and gracious, but they do not like, nay, they dread losing. It reflects upon their self-

concept in a far more dangerous manner than it does on those who
habitually lose and regard golf as only a game. Winners need to win
to reaffirm their personal worth. The tougher it gets, the harder they
try. They do not know when they have lost. Winning is like a drug
of which they need an injection from time to time.

Attitudes diverge significantly. Winners know how to keep their
arousal in check and, as a matter of conscious tactics, use as little
nervous energy as possible. They jealously guard a margin of safety,
a kind of mental reserve, a gold standard of the mind to tide them
over the rough patches. Any golfer will know the exhilaration
following a good round and the utter weariness following a bad one.
In the first, one's energy reserves were kept intact, while in the latter,
they have been exhausted. A good golfer uses mental energy to solve
complex problems. A poorer golfer uses it all the time. The good
golfer is less vulnerable in stressful situations; the poor golfer is at a
'high risk' even before the game has started. He burns himself out
in exhausting self-recriminations, negative expectations, endless
ruminations and anxious trepidations. A recent American study
revealed that winners:

- Suffer less anxiety,

- Are less given to attacks of rage or moodiness, and

- Adhere more rigorously to good ethical standards.

In golf there are only two deadly sins: **cheating** and **quitting**.
Cheating is a crime against all the other golfers in the field, quitting
is a crime against oneself.

Age is a significant factor. If success comes early, the idea of it
gets rooted in the mind. One learns to live with it and to expect it.
When the young Ballesteros, nineteen years of age, burst upon the
international scene, he did not expect to dominate the British
Open, nor did anyone else for that matter. There was this incredibly
good-looking Spaniard who seemed incapable of hitting a straight
shot, and distinctly preferred trees, sand and car parks to fairways.
He moved with the grace of a matador, and nothing befitted him

more than the thrilling manner of his recovery. By the time the Open was over and he finished second, the Ballesteros mania was firmly under way, and has lasted for twenty years now. With Seve, like Agassi and Tiger Woods, the crowds get involved. Since then, the pattern of his game has not changed: peaks and troughs, undisciplined and enthralling, sometimes exasperatingly sloppy and frequently inspiring. The end of his career was predicted often, but like the news of Mark Twain's death, it was greatly exaggerated. Even today, it would be a brave man who could say with any certainty that Ballesteros is finished.

Much has been written about the psychological management of defeat, how to recover confidence and heal a bruised spirit, but what about the victorious player and his over-swollen ego? Triumphs as well as defeats claim their victims. A minefield awaits the winner. Over-confidence is a double-edged sword, and one is never as vulnerable as when one is at the pinnacle of success.

After a defeat, the problem is well defined, and the main object is the restoration of confidence. Victory requires a mental adjustment of a more subtle nature to cope with life's new pressures:

(1) The fear of loneliness, and the inability or unwillingness to cope with resentment and jealousy.

(2) Success raises the stakes. One's own expectations and those of everyone around are higher. This puts enormous pressure on the winner to perform. It means gruelling work just to maintain present standards. Not everyone is prepared – or able – to make such an uncompromising investment in just one aspect of life.

(3) Guilt – the feeling that one ought not to win or that one does not deserve to win.

(4) No one can stay at the top forever. Failures trigger off powerful mechanisms of self-doubt which sabotage future victories.

The lonely champ...

There will be no easy matches ahead for the champion. The desire to win has been ignited and with it the fear of losing. In due course, titles have to be defended and there is the worry of not being able to repeat the coup. Toughest of all, the opponents have taken notice and, if they are worth their salt, are coming in pursuit. The winner has become a prime target.

Anonymity is a great asset. Success inspires more envy than admiration, and the winner may soon experience the chilly draught of social censure. Clubs have powerful means at their disposal – gossip, ridicule, isolation, humiliation, condemnation – and they use them ruthlessly. There may be grumbles about the handicap and oblique references to gamesmanship. If the winner is not the most popular member of the club, the subterranean campaign may rumble like an awakening volcano, threatening to pour boiling lava upon the new champion. But even if he is well liked, there will be disgruntled people who will find something to resent. This is human nature, and even on the international circuit, consistent winning inspires envy and hostility. In theory, the best person wins. In practice, some win too often. "When you're a champ, you're not one of the guys," said Nick Faldo in one of his most perceptive observations, when he became a subject of character assassination after winning 'too often'. The pressure proved too much even for him, and for a while he stopped winning. But being the great champion that he is, he came back.

Matches are zero-sum games: someone must win and someone must lose. Those who win are not necessarily the better players. There is no justice, only luck and survival. Survival of the winners and survival of the losers. The ability to regroup and start again is vital to any sportsman, because sooner or later everyone samples the bitter pill of defeat. "Every man's got to figure to get beat some-time," said Joe Louis. Competitions can seriously damage one's health. If one cannot handle a blow, one should not enter the arena.

The worst possible scenario is to have a commanding lead and lose it to a relentless opponent. In the 1996 Toyota World Match-play at Wentworth, one can only guess at Steve Stricker's state of mind upon losing a six-shot lead to Ernie Els. Presumably, he had groaned in disappointment upon receiving the draw, wishing his opponent were someone else and not the defending champion. But he was resolved to acquit himself with honour against Ernie. He came prepared. I bet he did everything right, including an early night. Els, on the other hand, was more likely to let out a sigh of relief: "A tough opponent, of course, but all the same, a relatively easy match. A good warming-up for the tougher matches ahead," he must have mused. It turned out to be a very different match from the one either of them had anticipated. To finish six down after eighteen holes must have been a very cold shower indeed. After lunch Ernie arrived ready to defend his title in earnest. At Wentworth that afternoon not many were prepared to wager a bet that Steve Stricker would win the match.

It is better to be the underdog than the top dog, which is why good players find themselves struggling against lesser players. When a match is perceived to be unequal, the better player is under more pressure to win, while the weaker player has nothing to lose, but the defeat that he was expected to suffer in the first place. The underdog has a limited objective. All he wants is an honourable defeat, not a walkover. His attitude is, therefore, more relaxed and focused, which can lead to some surprising results.

Finally, does one play better for oneself, or for a team? "Vanity of vanities, saith the Preacher, vanity of vanities; all is vanity." No doubt golf is a highly individualistic game and personal ambition plays an important role. But one only needs to witness the passion and the commitment among the players of the Ryder Cup or the Solheim Cup to realise that a cause is far more inspiring than personal glory. The burning ambition not to let the team down overrides private quest for recognition. When no selfish gain is involved, the demons that plague golf are momentarily subdued. The enemy within is silenced and ego is allowed to play as though it underwent catharsis. Whether it is for a hospital, a school, your club or your country, one would play one's guts out with a degree of commitment which is not usual when only personal triumph is at stake.

But playing for a team is not always the same as playing for a cause. Cohesion is a cardinal factor in team performance. United we stand, divided we fall. In sports where mutual dependence is high, group cohesion is absolutely crucial. Golf, however, is not soccer. There is no mutual dependence and there is no division of labour. All the members of the team perform the same role, and the result is either a win or a loss. Margins matter less or not at all. At most, partners in pair competitions need to relate to one another, but even that is not always mandatory or even desirable.

Though the members of the team operate independently of each other, the morale of the team does influence individual perform- ance. If the team is down, the members still in contention will double their efforts to win. But when morale is poor, the spirited unity of purpose collapses and the players are mired in a morass of personal animosities and general discontent. Members of the team who deem themselves wronged in some way will have trouble functioning optimally, no matter how well they ordinarily play. David Gilford played poorly in the 1991 Ryder Cup not because he is a lousy player. If he had been a lousy player, he would not have been in the team. He played poorly because Nick Faldo treated him like second rate. Had he played with someone more tolerant, he might have recovered his form, but playing with the thunderously silent and disapproving Nick in a major tournament proved too much.

Success is a balance between:

- The **motivation** to win,
- The **ability** to play,
- The **difficulty** of the task, and
- The imponderable matter of **luck**.

Every triumph has an element of luck. The curious thing is, that Lady Luck comes squarely and more than a trifle unfairly on the side of the winner. That is not to say that the match is won because of luck. The point is that it would have been won anyway, but luck makes it easy.

I bet you have been in matches, where an opponent's ball mysteriously disappeared after landing safely in the middle of the fairway. Or where a ball landed in a bunker, only to hit a stone which should not have been there in the first place, and flew straight to the flag. Or a top which sent the ball scuttling 150 yards to drop in for a birdie. Or a shank into the woods which miraculously ended on the fairway, as though tossed back by a fairy.

I can clearly remember a match when an archangel must have come to my rescue. I was playing in an away match on a course I had never played before. One look at my opponent and my heart sank. She was one of those strong, tall, blond girls with a pony tail... For her the ditch was not in play, but my ball went straight into it. A penalty shot. My next shot ended in a bunker, where I took two further shots. I found myself on the green for six while my opponent was a few yards away for two. She stooped to tidy up some leaves and twigs. I do not know whether she expected me to concede the hole, but she took her time. Suddenly the ball moved. She looked up in horror and dutifully counted three. The chip, when it finally came, went into a hollow. Stony faced she raised her club like an axe and gave the ball a solid whack, which buried it completely. In truth, we were both stunned. A few holes later, she needed a putt for a win. She was walking on a level green, when she tripped and kicked her ball. Another hole lost. And so it went on till the bitter end.

No one has tried to quantify the role of luck but few will dispute it. There are numerous examples but no logical explanations, so I will stick to the obvious one that Fortuna favours the winners. Nor am I alone in this belief. All golfers are deeply superstitious, and many are true believers. Bible Studies have been a regular feature of the PGA Tour for years, and the likes of Paul Azinger and Bernard Langer are regular attenders. All golfers have fetishes and swear by a certain type of ball and equipment. They dress with a certain symbolic flair to cultivate an image and keep the forces of evil at bay. Each has a secret mascot and, if his behaviour is not always whiter than white, he will say a prayer and, unlike Bernard Shaw, will resist temptation on the night before the tournament starts.

SUMMARY 9: WINNERS AND LOSERS

1. High self-efficacy is a necessary but not a sufficient condition for winning.

2. Winners are committed, prefer tough goals, never give-up and attribute both success and failure to the effort they put in.

3. Losers select easier goals, are more anxious, tend to tank, and believe that success and failure depend on ability alone.

4. Winning is a virtuous circle: the more one wins and the younger one is when first winning, the better are the chances of future victories.

5. The pitfalls of winning are:
   - Over-confidence,
   - Ballooning future expectations,
   - The fear of losing,
   - The glare of publicity, and
   - The crippling effect of envious others.

6. The nightmare scenario is to be in a winning position and lose.

7. Luck favours the winners.

Still climbing...

Glossary

Afferent. Sensory nerves which convey impulses from nerve organs and other receptors to the brain or spinal cord.

Arousal. Mobilisation of energy for action.

Autonomic nervous system. The part of the nervous system responsible for the control of body functions that are not consciously directed.

Carré breathing. Inhale/block/exhale/block to an equal count.

Concentration breath. A deep breath while focusing on one thought or word.

Deep breath. Filling with air the whole body cavity from the abdomen to the shoulders, followed by slow exhaling which empties the lungs of the last residue of air.

Differential relaxation. A basic technique which involves distinguishing between participating and non-participating muscles, and recognising different levels of tension in muscles.

Efferent. Motor nerves which convey impulses from the brain or spinal cord to muscles, glands and other effectors.

Emotionality. The physiological response to anxiety.

Evaluation apprehension. The concern about what others think of us.

Extravert. Outgoing, gregarious, dominant, aggressive, social-dependent personality.

Five-to-one breathing. A sequence of deep breaths, accompanied by visualisation of greater calm.

Focus: broad-narrow. The required attention style, depending on the amount of information needed for the task.

Focus: external-internal. The required attention style, depending on whether the cues are coming from the environment or from introspection.

Gamesmanship. The art of winning games by doubtful expedients without actually violating the rules.

Hyper-activation. A state of over-arousal.

Hypo-activation. A state of under-arousal.

Ideal-self. What one would like to be.

Imagery. Training programme which involves visualisation.

Introvert. Shy, self-sufficient, serious, inner-directed personality.

Inverted-U-Function. The function which depicts the relationship between arousal and performance.

One-to-one breathing. Inhaling to exhaling ratio of 1:2.

Optimal arousal. The level of arousal which produces best performance.

Outcome goals. What one sets out to achieve in terms of results and objectives.

Parasympathetic. The division of the autonomic nervous system responsible for relaxed state.

Passive progressive relaxation. Technique which involves releasing tension from all the muscles in the body.

Performance goals. Sets out how to achieve objectives.

Performance routines. The set of rituals the player employs before playing each shot.

Peripheral nervous system. All parts of the nervous system lying outside the central nervous system (brain and spinal cord).

Progressive muscular relaxation. A basic technique which involves tensing and relaxing in turn every muscle group in the body.

Self-efficacy. The confidence in one's ability to cope in specific situations.

Self-esteem. How one feels about oneself.

Self-image. What one knows about oneself.

Self-talk. Training programme which involves altering negative mental states.

Simulation. Training programme which involves mental representation of the anticipated situation.

Somatic. The voluntary muscles. Also, physiological state.

State anxiety. Anxiety which is precipitated by a threat.

Stress inoculation. Preventive training programme, designed to provide immunisation against stressors.

Sympathetic. The division of the autonomic nervous system responsible for fight and flight.

Trait anxiety. The propensity to be anxious.

Worry. The cognitive aspect of anxiety.

Further Reading

Self Hypnosis,
Brian M Alman and Peter Lambrou (Souvenir Press 1993).

The Ultimate Encyclopedia of Golf,
Ted Barrett and Michael Hobbs (Hodder and Stoughton 1996).

Assessing Coping Strategies,
Charles S. Carver et al (JOURNAL OF PERSONALITY AND SOCIAL
PSYCHOLOGY, 1989, VOL. 56, 2, 267-283).

Cognitive Psychology,
Michael W. Eysenck and Mark T Keane (LEA 1990).

Know Your Own Personality,
H.J. Eysenck and Glenn Wilson (Penguin Books 1975).

A Good Walk Spoiled,
John Feinstein (Warner Books 1995).

The Inner Game of Golf,
W. Timothy Gallwey (Pan Books 1981).

Understanding Psychological Preparation for Sport,
Lew Hardy, Graham Jones and Daniel Gould (John Wiley
& Sons 1996).

Stress and Performance in Sport,
Graham Jones and Lew Hardy (John Wiley & Sons 1990).

The New Toughness Training for Sports,
James E. Loehr (Plume Book 1995).

Competitive Anxiety in Sport,
R Martens et al (Human Kinetics, Champaign 1990).

In Pursuit of Excellence,
Terry Orlick (Leisure Press 1990).

Golf's Mental Hazards,
Alan Shapiro (Fireside 1996).

The Guinness Book of Golf,
Peter Smith and Keith Mackie (Guinness Publishing 1992).

Sport Psychology,
Daniel L. Wann (Prentice Hall 1997).

Applied Sport Psychology,
Jean M. Williams (Mayfield Publishing Company 1993).

To order further copies, write, Fax or telephone
Four Winds, PO Box 87, Godalming, Surrey GU7 2XY
Fax 01483 811196
Telephone 01483 811196 or 01483 811878

Please send me .... copies of Minding Your Golf, at £8.50 per copy.
Please add £1.45 for postage and packaging.

I enclose cheque/postal order payable to Four Winds Distributors for £ ....

Subject to availability, every effort will be made to despatch your copy as
soon as possible. Delivery guaranteed within 15 days, while stock lasts.